Footprints in the Ganges

佛　　陀

Footprints
in the
Ganges

The Buddha's Stories on
Cultivation and Compassion

By Venerable Master Hsing Yun

Published by Buddha's Light Publishing, Los Angeles

By Venerable Master Hsing Yun
Cover designed by Wilson Yau
Book designed by Wan Kha Ong and John Gill

Published by Buddha's Light Publishing
3456 S. Glenmark Drive,
Hacienda Heights, CA 91745, U.S.A.
Tel: (626) 923-5144
Fax: (626) 923-5145
E-mail: itc@blia.org
Website: www.blpusa.com

Printed in Taiwan.

Library of Congress Cataloging-in-Publication Data

Xingyun, da shi.
  Footprints in the Ganges / by Hsing Yun.
     p. cm.
  Translations of selections from Chinese.
  ISBN 978-1-932293-35-7
  1. Gautama Buddha. 2. Buddhism--Doctrines. I. Title.

  BQ9800.F6392X55435 2009
  294.3'4432--dc22

                                   2009011182

Acknowledgements

We received a lot of help from many people and we want to thank them for their efforts in making the publication of this book possible. We especially appreciate Venerable Tzu Jung, the Chief Executive of the Fo Guang Shan International Translation Center (F.G.S.I.T.C.), Venerable Hui Chi, Abbot of Hsi Lai Temple, and Venerable Yi Chao, Director of F.G.S.I.T.C. for their support and leadership; the volunteers from IBPS in Austin, Denver, Los Angeles, Toronto, Vancouver, London and Manchester for their translation; Louvenia Ortega and John Gill for their editing; Michael Tran and Wan Kah Ong for proofreading and preparing the manuscript for publication; and Wilson Yau for his cover design. Our appreciation also goes to everyone who has supported this project from its conception to its completion.

Contents

Footprints in the Ganges

INTRODUCTION

The Dharma, the teachings of the Buddha, has helped people find happiness and live better lives for over twenty-five hundred years. The Buddha's teachings have been able to endure and remain relevant because they are concerned with the unchanging aspects of the human condition: the need for comfort and happiness in thus uncertain and changing world, the need to understand ourselves and find meaning in our lives, and the need to be free from the suffering and mental afflictions that constrain us. The Dharma is for all times and all places because it communicates directly to who we are.

While the Dharma has come to our modern times across centuries and touched every continent of the earth we live on, it can be traced back to a single time when the Buddha first turned the wheel of the Dharma in the Deer Park near the city of Benares in what is now India. For forty-nine years the Buddha taught the Dharma throughout India to people from every walk of life, showing to all those he encountered the path to liberation. His legacy has continued to this day, as the lives that he touched have rippled outwards— with each generation sharing the Dharma anew.

While the Dharma wheel continues to turn, there is something special to be gained from looking at the moment when it first began, from knowing the life of the Buddha. The Buddha did not just teach the Dharma to correspond to the human condition; he taught the Dharma to individual people with respect to their own circumstances. The Buddha was a perfect teacher who taught each person he encountered in such a way that they could understand. The universal nature of the Dharma is born out of these individual encounters. While the Dharma transcends time and space, it is always spoken for a specific time, a specific place, and to individuals.

Footprints in the Ganges is about those individuals. It is a collection of stories from the Buddha's life: some depict the peaceful lives of the Buddha's disciples, some are full of drama and conflict, and some are even funny. What they all share is that they have something to teach us— something we can take away and carry with us so that we can live happier, more peaceful, and more compassionate lives.

Footprints in the Ganges is a translation of a collection of stories from the Buddha's life by Venerable Master Hsing Yun. These stories were adapted from the Chinese Buddhist scriptures and written in modern Chinese so that everyone could have access to the stories from the Buddhist scriptures in clear, accessible language. The goal of the English translation of *Footprints in the Ganges* has been the same: to present these classic stories in a warm and natural way. The stories have been grouped into ten sections meant to roughly correspond to the experience of a person encountering Buddhism for the first time. First we enter the Dharma and experience the moment when we see or hear about Buddhism for the first time, and want to learn how it can help us. We are moved by the Buddha's kindness and compassion, and begin to look for answers in the world around us. We come to understand the law of karma: that everything arises due to causes and conditions, and that every action has an effect. As our confidence grows we learn from the Buddha's life and his example, and are amazed by the miracles of both his supernatural powers and his teaching. We take what we have learned and enter the world, living in community with all living beings, and learn from Buddhist monastics and other practitioners in our community. We develop a Buddhist practice, and look for opportunities in each moment to become more generous, more compassionate, and more wise. While we are on this path we may stray along the way, but each minor misstep is an opportunity to regain our focus— we admit our faults and resolve to practice better in the future.

It is my sincerest hope that these stories become favorites, not only to be enjoyed in this book, but to be shared and retold. It is in sharing stories like these, of the lives that the Buddha touched and those that he liberated from suffering, that the Dharma has come to us today, and it is in sharing and telling stories of our own that will allow it to go forward for years to come.

Part One:

Entering the Dharma

For every journey there is a first step, and the first step on the Buddhist path is entering the Dharma: the moment of inspiration when a person knows that he or she can truly find happiness, and that the Buddha can show them the way. These stories show the Buddha as a great leader, unwilling to leave anyone behind as he leads sentient beings to enter the Dharma.

The Pride of the Brahmans

Once, the Buddha was residing and teaching with his disciples beside a lake just outside the city of Jampa. Jampa was a booming, densely populated city where the standard of living was high and stable. The city had been given to the Brahmans by King Prasenajit, where they had lived for seven generations. The Brahmans were honorable, respectable and educated citizens. They were learned in many subjects and excelled in the practice of divination and sacrificial rites. Through their good conduct they had amassed five hundred well-trained followers.

When the residents of Jampa learned that the Buddha was staying at the nearby lake, many took their elders and children with them and headed toward the lake to get a glimpse of the famous and lucid teacher. They wanted to see the holy appearance of the Buddha and to hear the Buddha teach the Dharma.

While the leader of the Brahmans was overlooking Jampa from a high platform he saw waves and waves of people rushing toward the lake. He asked the attendant standing next to him, "What is going on over there?"

The attendant replied, "Everyone wants to go and pay homage to the Buddha."

He then gathered his five hundred disciples to go and pay homage to the Buddha. As they were departing, a Brahman asked, "Teacher, you gathered us here on such short notice; is there an emergency? Are you going to take us to meet another teacher?"

The Brahman leader replied, "I just heard that the Buddha is residing near the lake outside the city. The Buddha is an awakened one who teaches the Truth to help sentient beings free themselves from affliction. It is such a rare opportunity for the Buddha to be teaching near here, so we should all go and pay homage to him."

One of the Brahman followers said, "Teacher, you should not pay homage to him! You are a Brahman, and the master of our city. He should come to pay homage to you! You are an honorable, highly cultivated, and persuasive sage. It is the Buddha who should come see you."

The Brahman leader told his disciples, "Although I am worthy of all the accolades you bestow upon me, I cannot compare to the Buddha. I should go see him. The Buddha was born in a royal family. He has a dignified appearance and a kind and gentle voice. He is completely free from the bondage of the passions and is the leader of all human beings. King Prasenajit and King Bimbisara have much respect for him, and make offerings to him. I should be the one to pay homage to him." After the five hundred followers heard what the Brahman leader had to say, they were speechless. They all departed to see the Buddha.

On the way, the Brahman leader grew worried. He thought to himself, "In a little while, I will meet with the Buddha. If I do not ask my questions properly, the Buddha may reproach me and point out my mistakes. Others who are present might think that I am a foolish person; this may affect my ability to lead the people of my city. If I cannot answer his questions, will I not be exposing my own ignorance?"

The Buddha was aware of his concerns. Thus, when the Brahmans arrived, the Buddha greeted them kindly and compassionately. Once everyone was seated, the Buddha asked the Brahman leader, "Please tell me what qualities one must possess to become a Brahman?"

As soon as he heard the Buddha's question, his worries dissipated. He thought, "This is absolutely marvelous. The Buddha is truly considerate. He must have known my worries, and asked me a simple question."

As the Brahman leader sat solemnly, he looked around, smiled, and replied, "There are five prerequisites for becoming a Brahman. First, one has to be born into the Brahman caste. Second, one must be fluent in all kinds of subjects and be able to practice divination and conduct sacrificial rites. Third, one must look dignified and proper. Fourth, one must be able to uphold the precepts. Fifth, one must be wise."

Then, the Buddha said, "Very good. Of these five prerequsites, can you still be a Brahman if you only have the last four?"

The Brahman leader answered, "Yes, one can still be a Brahman with the last four prerequisites."

"How about with the last three prerequisites?"

"Yes, Lord Buddha. One can still be a Brahman with the last three prerequisites."

"How about one less?"

"Yes, as long as one can uphold the precepts and is wise, one can still be a Brahman." As soon as the Brahman leader finished talking, his five hundred followers were shocked and expressed their disagreement.

The Buddha addressed the five hundred Brahmans in attendance, "If you feel that your leader does not have a proper appearance, has not been born into the Brahman caste, is not articulate, and is not qualified to discuss this with me, you may speak out. If you agree that he has the proper appearance, has been born into the Brahman caste, is articulate, and is able to discuss this with me, please listen to us."

The Brahman leader was ashamed of his followers and told the Buddha, "Lord Buddha, I know how to teach them." He then turned to the five hundred Brahmans and said, "Seated here is my nephew Angamana. Except for the Buddha, his dignified appearance is second to none. If he goes out today and commits murder and arson, can he still be a Brahman?" With this rebuttal, his disciples were silenced.

The Buddha then started to talk, "Very good. Of the two qualities you named, upholding the precepts and wisdom, can one still be a Brahman if one is absent?"

"Impossible, Lord Buddha. The precepts are wisdom and wisdom is the precepts. You cannot be lacking in either."

After the Buddha heard his reply, he said cheerfully, "You are absolutely right. As you said, if one upholds the precepts, one possesses wisdom. To have wisdom is to uphold the precepts. The precepts can purify wisdom and wisdom can purify the precepts. It is like washing hands. Both hands must be rubbed together to be clean . The left hand cleans the right hand and the right hand cleans the left hand." The Buddha then gave a teaching on upholding the precepts and the Brahman leader was so moved by the Buddha that he took refuge. He became a lay Buddhist follower and mindfully kept the five precepts.

Prostitutes Receive the Precepts

In the Sravasti, there lived a wealthy nobleman who had three sons who loitered in the brothels and spent money every day without restraint. Day after day, the wealth of the nobleman was running out.

Worried, the nobleman pleaded with the king, "King, those prostitutes have seduced my sons and brought my family to ruin! You should execute them so that no other families will be destroyed."

The king told the nobleman, "I have received the Buddha's precepts; I don't even hurt worms or ants, how could I hurt a human being? I have heard that the Buddha will teach anyone and that he is very resourceful in teaching his students. Let us go and ask the Buddha for help."

The king and the nobleman went to pay homage to the Buddha and asked the Buddha to teach the Dharma to the prostitutes. The Buddha gathered all the prostitutes in the city and gave a teaching on the five aggregates, "The body is made of the four elements: wind, fire, water, and earth. It is full of many filthy substances like puss, mucus, saliva, blood, sweat, stool, and urine. It doesn't matter how gorgeous you may be, it does not change this fact. If you are caught up in the illusion of beauty, then one is no different than an old elephant stuck in a marsh, sinking deeper and deeper."

The prostitutes listened to the Buddha's teachings and were so ashamed they began to cry, "Oh, Lord Buddha! You are right! We dress up our dirty bodies to seduce people. We're tired of living this way, but we're filthy like used rags. How can we make ourselves pure again?"

The Buddha comforted them and said, "Do not give up on yourselves. It does not matter what one's past is; as long as one is truly remorseful of past wrongs, one can still become awakened and attain liberation. Dirty clothes become clean through washing, filthy bodies become clean through bathing. In the same way, the Dharma can purify the defiled mind. Even the most polluted stream is purified by the ocean once it flows into it. If you have faith in the Dharma, its water can definitely cleanse your defiled mind and help you all to attain awakening and liberation."

The Buddha's words gave confidence to the prostitutes to reform and mend their ways. They all pleaded with the Buddha to transmit the five precepts to them. They vowed to stay away from their immoral way of life and became lay Buddhist followers.

Even the gravest crime can be purified by sincere repentance. Past wrongs can then be absolved without a trace. The most dreadful thing is when one gives up on oneself and willingly wallows in despair. The difference between the defiled and the pure lies in a single thought.

Afflictions Like Tree Shadows

The Nirgranthas were one of the six sects of wanderers in ancient India. Today we refer to this group as the followers of Jainism.

One day, a Nirgrantha came to the sangha to debate with the Venerable Maudgalyayana. The Buddha happened to see him and asked him about his intention. He said, "Lord Buddha! I have heard that Maudgalyayana has great supernatural powers and is a great debater. I made a special trip today to have a session with him."

"Nirgrantha, what is it you want to know?"

"Lord Buddha, I heard that many monks do not practice according to the monastic rules, and frequently experience ignorance and afflictions. Why not let them follow our religious teaching, so that they may attain awakening?"

"Nirgrantha, it is normal for monks to experience ignorance and afflictions. A standing tree cast a shadow. But, if the tree is axed down, will the shadow exist on its own?"

"Lord Buddha, since the tree has fallen, the shadow vanishes with it."

"Nirgrantha, this is true. If the monks practice according to the monastic rules, their ignorance and afflictions will completely disappear, just like the shadow that disappears as a tree falls. The obstacles that arise during Dharma practice can be seen as tests that one must pass during one's spiritual quest. If the monks practice persistently, they will certainly attain awakening."

The Buddha then taught the Nirgrantha the Three Dharma Seals, the Four Noble Truths, and the Twelve Links of Dependent Origination. Having listened to the teachings of the Buddha, the Nirgrantha instantly achieved higher understanding. Without hesitation he expressed his heartfelt remorse to the Buddha, renounced his prior belief, took refuge in the Triple Gem, and became a member of the sangha.

The afflictions of the mind are like the leaves on a tree, and ignorance is the roots. No matter how well the leaves flourish, if we eradicate ignorance, then the trunk and all the leaves will wither. Removing the root of our ignorance is the first priority of practice. Once it is subdued, all the rest of our afflictions will disappear. The Buddha is skillful in adopting similes to illustrate his teaching, as one can see in the twelve divisions of the Buddhist canon. In this story, the simile of a tree shadow is used to help us understand the nature of afflictions. It also shows the Buddha's open-mindedness toward people and that he never insisted that his disciples instantly attain perfection.

Confronting Nirgrantha

Once there lived an elder who was the richest man in the city of Suddpara. Although he cultivated diligently, he could not recognize true teachings from false ones, and became the disciple of a recluse named Nirgrantha and made offerings to him everyday.

The Buddha had compassion for the elder and decided to teach him the Dharma. The Buddha brought his disciples to Suddpara. When Nirgrantha learned that the Buddha would be arriving soon, he was fearful and fretted, "When the Buddha arrives, everyone will be converted by the wisdom and virtue of the Buddha. They will leave me and no longer make offerings to me. What can I do? I have to think of a way to stop this from happening."

Nirgrantha told the elder, "The Buddha is an unfilial son who has forsaken his parents. He does not tend to the affairs of his country, and just travels from place to place. Wherever he passes, crops do not grow and people are hungry. We should be cautious."

"What can we do to prevent this from happening?"

"I know the Buddha likes rustic places with trees and streams. If there are such places outside the city, we should cut down the trees and dump dirt into the streams and ponds. When they enter the city, we should brandish our weapons to stop them from entering. Then I will use mantras to drive them away. This is the only way to be rid of them." The elder dared not disobey the orders of Nirgrantha, so he then notified all the residents to do as Nirgrantha had instructed.

Before long, the Buddha and his disciples arrived at the outskirts of the city. They saw that all the trees had been felled and the clear beautiful streams and ponds were littered with trash. The scene was so desolate that the Buddha was deeply saddened.

He used his supernatural power to restore all the trees. The streams and ponds were once again filled with water so clean and pure that the bottom could be seen through. He then turned all the brick walls into clear glass blocks so that people in the city could see what had happened. Witnessing this, the elder and other residents were naturally drawn to the Buddha to hear him teach, "Elder, you have numerous blessings and a store of merit from the past. I have purposely come here to teach the Dharma to you. False ways can never be compared to righteous teachings. Not only will wrong views not lead you to heaven, you will fall into an unfortunate rebirth. Is it not a waste if we use our precious lives and our limited energy on the wrong path? If you can follow my teachings with the same devotion you once gave to Nirgrantha, you will attain great joy and wisdom."

When the elder and the other residents witnessed the supernatural power of the Buddha, they were already convinced. When they heard the teachings of the Buddha, they repented for what they had done. They were like children who, after having been bullied for a long time, had finally found their mothers. The elder was filled with reverence and appreciation. All that he could say was, "Lord Buddha, you are compassionate and wonderful!"

How can a weak, flickering light ever be as bright as the sun and the moon? During the Buddha's time, there were many teachers from other religions who came to challenge the Buddha. Yet the majestic Buddha was always able to show them the error of their ways and to help them repent and reform their misguided ways.

To Instruct and Guide Robbers

Once, there were five hundred robbers in Sravasti who had robbed the people of their valuables. The residents were so terrified that they would close the stores before dark and did not go out at night. The people feared the robbers as much as they feared tigers.

The king of Sravasti was worried and ordered his troops to arrest the five hundred robbers. Through great effort, the five hundred robbers were finally arrested. After their arrest, The king angrily said, "You're detestable, disturbing people by stealing their belongings! You deserve worse than one thousand death penalties and should be publicly executed!"

The five hundred robbers thought of the Buddha's compassion and loudly called out the his name while they were in prison. The Buddha heard the robbers' pleas and told Ananda, "I heard the five hundred robbers calling me and know that their kindness is growing. I love them compassionately, as much as I love all sentient beings. Go and tell the king that he should love his people as he loves his own son and not to kill the five hundred robbers."

Ananda took the Buddha's orders and went to the king to tell him what the Buddha had said. "King, the karmic consequences of even a single act of killing is great – if you kill the five hundred robbers, the misery that will result from that will be immeasurable. Please think very carefully about what you are going to do."

The king replied, "I have thought it over. If the Buddha can stop the robbers from stealing from my people, then I will release them."

Ananda gave the Buddha the king's message, and the Buddha said, "Ananda, I can make the robbers put an end to their misguided ways. Ask the king to show them mercy and I will make these men stop stealing."

Ananda walked to the execution square and said to the execution supervisor, "The Buddha has saved the robbers. You have been temporarily ordered not to kill them."

The king understood the Buddha's intention and released the robbers immediately, but left them bound by ropes. He ordered the robbers to be escorted to the Buddha. The Buddha intended to teach the Dharma to the robbers, so he began meditating. The five hundred robbers arrived under escort, and saw the Buddha's radiant appearance in the distance. Happiness arose in their minds, and the ropes that bound them suddenly loosened and fell to the ground. The robbers saw the Buddha as their savior and ran up to him to bow with gratitude.

The compassionate Buddha smiled, observed their establishment in the Dharma, and then taught them the Four Noble Truths of suffering, the cause of suffering, the cessation of suffering, and the path leading to the cessation of suffering. Afterwards, the Buddha asked them, "Do you want to join the sangha?" The robbers, all together answered, "We have endured so much suffering because we did not take the precepts before. Please accept us into your sangha." The Buddha nodded his head and smiled. The five hundred robbers had their heads shaved by Sariputra and entered the monastic life. They made vows to begin their lives anew.

It doesn't matter how depraved you are, as long as you repent and reform the Buddha will not give up on you.

The Mother of Demons

Once there was a woman named Hariti who would eat children. Though she loved her own children dearly, she would steal other people's children and feast upon them. All the parents who heard of her worried that they would lose their children someday.

Eventually, the Buddha heard of this woman and her monstrous appetite. The Buddha realized that she was not a human woman, but was an evil spirit who was the mother of five hundred demons. The Buddha instructed a monk to kidnap Hariti's youngest demon child and bring him to the monastery. Once Hariti realized her little boy was missing, she would not stop crying and refused to eat.

The Buddha called on Hariti and asked why she was distraught. She wiped her tears and told the Buddha that her beloved youngest son was missing.

The Buddha asked her when she had lost her son. She was shocked— she had lost him while she was stealing someone else's child. She realized that this was due to her own cruelty and wrongdoing. In profound remorse she bowed before the Buddha and begged for his help.

"Do you love your child?" the Buddha asked.

"Yes," Hariti replied, "I loved my youngest son the most. He never left my sight— I can't live without him!"

The Buddha saw this as an opportunity to teach her, "Now that you understand the unbearable pain and sorrow of losing a child and the suffering that you have caused others, do you still hope to find your child?"

"I will do anything as long as I can have my son back."

"I can help you find your child. Do you truly regret stealing other's children?"

"Yes! Please teach me, and I will always follow your teachings."

The Buddha then taught her the five precepts, "From now on, do not kill, do not steal, do not engage in sexual misconduct, do not lie, and do not consume intoxicants. Most of all, take care of all the children in the world with your compassionate maternal nature."

Hariti agreed, but asked the Buddha what she would do for food since she would no longer eat children.

"From now on," the Buddha said, "I will ask my monks to make an offering before they eat their alms food." At this Hariti accepted the Buddha's teaching and became a protector of all the children in the world. Even today, monastics always make an offering before their meal, in order to offer the meal to Hariti just as the Buddha taught.

Even the most evil demons will be able to transforms their wickedness when they are met with great compassion and become protector's for all living beings. Kindness has no enemy, great compassion is the ultimate virtue.

Refraining from Contempt

In the city of Kunala there lived an arrogant Brahman. He was born into a wealthy family and was blessed with both eloquence and good looks. People often thought that he must have done good deeds in his previous lives in order to have such good fortune. However, he was neither grateful for what he had in this life, nor respectful to his parents, teachers or elders.

When he heard that the Buddha was teaching at Jetavana Monastery a few miles outside of the city, he decided to go there to engage the Buddha in debate. He departed for Jetavana Monastery in a beautiful white horse-drawn carriage while a group of younger brahmans cheered while holding golden canopies and vases. Once he arrived, he came down from his carriage and entered the monastery. At this time the Buddha was in the middle of teaching, and did not pay any attention to him. The arrogant Brahman thought, "Since I arrived the Buddha didn't even look at me or acknowledge my presence! Maybe I should leave."

The Buddha was aware of the Brahman's intentions and immediately said to him, "Arrogant Brahman, you have come here to challenge me. Since you arrived your arrogance has only grown. Originally you came here to listen to the Dharma, and you should do so. I hope that you will realize the truth and abandon your contempt for others." Upon hearing this the Brahman thought that the Buddha must have supernatural powers since he knew his thoughts before he expressed them.

The Brahman began to question the Buddha. He spoke in verse:

> "Why refrain from contempt?
> Why cultivate the virtue of respect?
> What is the art of speaking well of others?
> What is a true offering?"

The Buddha responded with a verse of his own:

"Parents, teachers, and arhats should be respected
There is no stable, unchanging being.
To have contempt for others is unacceptable.
No one to give, no one to receive, and no gift are the
parts of true giving.
Keep the precepts, meditate and rid yourself of delusion.
We bow to the beings who hold these virtues."

The Brahman was so touched and convinced by Buddha's answer that he bowed before the Buddha and asked to be admitted into the sangha. Soon, the Brahman followed in the Buddha's footsteps and became an arhat.

The Way Leads to Long Life

There was once a large kingdom where all the citizens were members of a certain cult that believed in blood sacrifice.

One day, the king's mother became very ill. Upon the advice of the Brahmans, the king was told to sacrifice a teenager and one hundred elephants, horses, cows, and goats to the gods to cure his mother's illness.

The Buddha felt compassion for the ignorant king who would sacrifice so many lives, so he and his disciples set forth for his kingdom. On the way to the kingdom, the Buddha and his disciples met the king and his Brahmans who were leading a crowd of people and animals. The king could see light shining from the Buddha's body, so he got off his carriage, and bowed to the Buddha.

The Buddha asked the king where he was going, and the king replied, "My mother has been ill for a long time. After seeing all the best doctors, no one was able to cure her. Now I am taking these animals to be sacrificed to the gods, in hopes that my mother's illness will soon be cured."

The Buddha told the king, "Everything in this world is related to karma. In order to harvest crops, one must work hard in the field. To get rich, one must practice virtue and generosity. To have a long life, one must not kill. In order to gain wisdom one must study diligently. Sacrificing life goes against the gods, who cherish all life. The gods live in elegant palaces decorated with precious jewels. All their food manifests by itself as needed. Why would they want a bloody human sacrifice? Rich people do not want to eat the coarse food of the poor. Therefore, killing many lives to save one is a very ignorant action."

After listening to the Buddha's advice, the king and his two hundred Brahmans felt ashamed of their ignorance and asked to take refuge in the Buddha and become his disciples. Later, they sincerely invited the Buddha and his disciples to the palace for a meal offering and to give teachings to the king's mother. After listening to the teachings, the king's mother suddenly felt much better and soon the illness was gone. From then on, the king applied the Dharma to the running of his country, and his kingdom gradually became more prosperous and strong.

A long life comes from compassion, while a short life is caused by killing. Only when one is compassionate and decides not to kill can one receive the fruit of long life. Taking life to extend your own, is like pouring oil into water and expecting the oil to sink to the bottom. It's absolutely impossible. Therefore, when we celebrate our birthdays, remember not to harm any sentient beings. Such actions cannot grant us longer lives, but instead will only lead to a short life.

The Impermanence of Life

In Rajagrha, there was a non-Buddhist ascetic who had heard that, since the Buddha went to Sravasti to spread the Dharma, the citizens there had become virtuous, polite, and reasonable people. He had great respect for the Buddha and was eager to learn his teachings. He gave up his ascetic practices and traveled the long distance to Sravasti to visit the Buddha. Before he met the Buddha, he saw something very strange.

Since Sravasti was in a tropical climate, there were many poisonous snakes. When a person was bitten by one of these poisonous snakes, he would die shortly thereafter. As a result, many people died of snake bites.

As the ascetic neared Sravasti, he saw a father and son working in a field. Suddenly, a snake shot out of the tall grasses and bit the son. The young man soon died from the poison. Upon seeing the death of his son, the old man did not show any grief, but simply continued working.

The ascetic looked on in wonder and asked the old man, "Was that your son?"

The old man answered, "Yes, he was my son."

"If he was your son, why are you not sad?"

"Why should I be? Everyone has to die eventually. Death is a law of nature. It's only a matter of time before we all die. If my son accumulated merit in this life, he will have a good rebirth. Otherwise, he will have a bad rebirth. Crying for him is not going to help."

The old man then asked the perplexed newcomer, "Are you going into the city? If so, can you do me a favor?"

"What can I do for you?"

"When you go into the city, please tell my family that my son has died of a snake bite and that they only need to send one lunch for me. My house is the second one on the first street to your right past the gates of the city."

The ascetic thought to himself, "This old man is a callous person. Not only was he not sad, all he could think of was his lunch. What kind of father is he?"

Once he entered the city, the ascetic found the old man's house and gave his wife the sad news. The woman thanked him but did not show any sorrow either. The man asked, "Aren't you sad that your son is dead?"

The mother answered, "My son decided to come to my family. Now that he is gone, I can't make him stay any longer. He was just like a guest who came to stay for the night and in the morning must be on his way. This is the relationship between a mother and a son. The son has to follow his own karma, and his mother can't help him."

The man thought to himself, "What a stupid and unfeeling couple!"

Meanwhile the sister of the dead man came into the front room. The ascetic asked the sister, "Your brother died of snake poison. Are you sad?"

"Why should I be sad?" Brothers and sisters are like timber traveling together along a river. If the wind blows them apart, they have to separate. They can't travel together forever. Karma brought us together as brother and sister in this life. But we all die at different times. Now that his life has ended, what can I do to change things?"

At that moment, another woman entered and remarked casually, "Oh, my husband is dead."

The ascetic turned to the young man's wife, and asked, "Your husband is dead! why aren't you sad?"

The wife answered calmly, "Husbands and wives are like birds in the sky. We happen to rest on the same branch for the night, but we must go our separate ways in the morning. We each have different karma that determines our destination. No one can change this."

By now the ascetic was completely perplexed. When he saw a servant of the man who died, he asked, "Your young master is dead, why aren't you crying?"

To his surprise, the servant answered, "Everyone in this household came together due to the force of karma. I am like a calf following the cows. When the cow is killed, the calf's crying is not going to help."

After the man heard everyone in the household, he became very upset. He regretted he even took the time to visit this family. He traveled a long distance to learn the Buddha's teachings because he had heard that the people of Sravasti obeyed their parents and respected the Buddha, the Dharma and the sangha. Now he found out that the people of Sravasti had no love or compassion. How could he learn anything from these people?

Since he was already inside the city, he thought that he might as well see the Buddha before returning to his own country, so he went to Jetavana Monastery and asked to see the Buddha. After the man bowed respectfully to the Buddha, he sat to one side but did not ask any questions. The Buddha knew what was bothering him but still asked, "What has made you so upset?"

The man answered, "I am unhappy because what I saw was not what I expected."

"Why does this bother you?" Being upset is not going to change anything."

The man raised his head and answered, "I came from far away to this place because I heard that through your teaching the people of Sravasti follow the true Dharma. I did not expect to meet these cold-hearted people!" He then told the Buddha about the behavior of the farmer's family. He thought this kind of loveless behavior should not happen in a country with the Buddha's teaching.

The Buddha smiled and told him, "Your expectations are typical, but the law of nature is not always consistent with our expectations. Impermanence is the law of nature. The most important thing is to practice and purify our nature, so that it will be in accordance with reality. The farmer's family did not act inappropriately, they simply understand that life is impermanent. No one can keep his body forever, regardless of whether he is a sage or a common person. This is the law of nature, and it stretches across the past, present, and future. Once someone dies, crying is not going to help. Whenever there is birth, there will be death. Since we do not understand the true nature of things, we celebrate birth and feel sorrow at death. This is why we continue to stay in this never-ending cycle of birth and death."

The ascetic heard the Buddha's teaching and attained awakening. He took refuge in the Buddha and became a monk who practiced diligently.

What is the Way?

Mahasatya the Nirgrantha was an elder Brahman with five hundred followers. He was very conceited and looked down on everyone. He would wear iron plates around his chest and abdomen, and when asked why he wore them, he would answer, "I am worried that my wisdom and talent may flow out of my body."

One day he learned that the Buddha had been teaching the Dharma and winning followers everywhere, and that he had become respected and supported by many. Mahasatya became very envious of the Buddha, so he traveled to Jetavana Monastery with his followers to challenge the Buddha.

"Tell me," Mahasatya asked, "What do you mean by 'the Way?' What do you mean by 'wisdom?' Who can be called an 'elder?' What does it mean to be 'dignified?' Who can be called a 'sage?' Who can be called a 'monk?' What is meant by 'virtue?' What does it mean to 'attain the Way?' What does it mean to 'uphold the precepts?' If you can answer all these questions, I shall be willing to follow your lead."

Fully aware of Mahasatya's ill intended visit, the Buddha kindly and calmly answered his questions one by one as follows:

"The Buddha Way is to learn diligently and earnestly, conduct oneself honestly, be pure and free from the defilements in body and in mind, and to fullly commit to cultivating supramundane wisdom.

"Having wisdom is avoiding the display of oratory and debating skills, living without terror or fear, keeping the heart magnanimous and free, and discerning the truth and holding to it without hesitation.

"One cannot be called an elder simply because of one's age. If a person holds the truth dearly in his heart, treats all creatures with loving kindness, is wise and sagacious, and gains a heart as clear as a mirror through his complete understanding, that person can be addressed as an elder.

"Dignity does not refer to having a dignified appearance. If a person leaves his evil habits behind, stops being greedy, cultivates wisdom, and eliminates hatred, then he is a dignified person.

"Being a sage goes beyond just having one's hair and beard shaved. A true sage is generous and does nothing unwholesome, sets his mind at rest, ends all desires, and resolves to teach the truth.

"Being a monk is more than just carrying a bowl and collecting alms. One who abandons all defilements, diligently cultivates pure conduct, promotes wisdom, and refutes falsehood can be called a true monk.

"Virtue does not belong to him who promotes himself with empty words, or to him who applies himself insincerely. All these people have is the appearance of virtue. Virtue means having a pure mind, few worldly needs, being content easily, being free from desire, and delighting in peace and tranquility.

"Attaining the Way is more than performing an isolated act of generosity. Attaining the Way means liberating all sentient beings in the universe and treating friends and foes equally.

"Upholding the precepts is more than just saying a few words. Even if one learns only a little, when one obeys and practices the teachings one has received and guards one's practice without retreat until the end of life, then one has truly upheld the precepts.

After having heard the Buddha's teaching, Mahasatya the

Nirgrantha and his five hundred followers set their arrogance aside, kept their promise, and sincerely paid homage to their new teacher, the Buddha.

From the Buddha's reply, one can see that spiritual practice is more than the observance of rules in their various forms. It involves the more important aspect of personal commitment, diligent practice, and conscientious application.

A Hundred Year Old Man Becomes a Monk

In Rajagrha there lived a man named Shihlibiti who was one hundred years old. He was told that if he renounced the household life and became a monk he would gain boundless merit, so he soon decided to ordain and follow the Buddha. Shihlibiti then went to the Bamboo Grove to seek out the sangha of monks. Since the Buddha was away, Shihlibiti went to see Sariputra, Mahakasyapa, Upali, Aniruddha and other prominent disciples. Despite his great faith and willingness, Shihlibiti's request to join the sangha was rejected by all of them, due to his age and frailty.

Greatly disappointed, Shihlibiti walked away from the quiet monastery. Soon he broke down and began to cry. At that moment the Buddha appeared before him, emitting immense light. The Buddha exhibited various magnificent dignified features. As if awakened from a dream, Shihlibiti frantically knelt down to pay homage to the Buddha.

The Buddha asked compassionately, "Why is it that you are crying so hard?"

"Lord Buddha, what have I done that is so wrong that

Sariputra and the other monks will not accept my ordination? I am crying because I feel so sad and heartbroken."

The Buddha comforted the old man with kindness, "Do not be sad and cease your worries. I welcome all people, both old and young without distinction. Although an elderly person cannot be a missionary, it is still good to be a monk so one can be disciplined and diligently practice. I will be very happy if you became a monk." Thus, Shihlibiti followed the Buddha back to the Bamboo Grove.

After the elderly man became a monk, he practiced diligently and became an arhat after only a short time.

One needs to learn the Buddhist teachings and cultivate oneself as soon as possible. Do not put off learning and cultivating until old age, otherwise one is wasting one's precious life.

Turning Over A New Leaf

When the Buddha was teaching the Dharma at Rajagrha, the king, his ministers and thousands upon thousands of people became followers of the Buddha, rapidly forming a growing group of firm believers.

Devadatta could not contain his anger when he saw the Buddha's glorious achievements. With growing jealousy and hostility, he began to make plans to rid himself of the Buddha.

He used a large amount of money to hire five hundred skillful Brahman archers. He said to them, "I despise the Buddha, for he bewitches the king and his subjects with magic and paralyzes them to obey him. All the people devote themselves to following his teachings, while I look like a fool before his magic. Tomorrow, when the Buddha is out teaching the Dharma and making his alms round, he will pass by these woods. I want you to hide here and shoot him down when he passes. When your mission is completed, you shall be handsomely rewarded."

The next day the archers hid in the woods as planned and waited to ambush the Buddha. When they saw the Buddha walking towards the woods with peaceful steps, the archers shot all at once. Surprisingly, the hundreds of sharp arrows became fragrant lotus flowers as they touched the body of the Buddha. He was not injured at all.

Terrified at witnessing the Buddha's mighty supernatural powers, the five hundred archers immediately dropped their bows and arrows and knelt down before the Buddha, repenting, "Lord Buddha, save us! Devadatta used our greed to deceive us. He ordered us to harm you. Our crimes are as high as Mount Sumeru. Only your great compassion can save us." They then burst into tears.

The Buddha realized that their confessions were true and said to them gently, "Do not be afraid. Wrongdoing lacks an independent self-nature. It is caused by our bad karma. When one overcomes improper desire and wrong ideas, all defilements will disappear naturally. If we can control our desires and put an end to our ill intentions before they sprout and grow, we will not commit any wrongdoings. Even if people are guilty of wrongdoings, as long as they have the courage to repent their former actions and reform themselves, they will have a chance at redemption. You attempted to harm me, but I do not bear any grudges. From now on, it is very important to cultivate yourselves by following the right path with your best effort."

The five hundred archers calmed down and were cheerfully

encouraged. One archer said to the Buddha, "Lord Buddha, you are merciful just like a kind parent who will forgive all the misdeeds of a child instead of abandoning him. We wish to follow you and leave home to cultivate ourselves and do good deeds for the benefit of all sentient beings. Under your guidance, we will not lose our way again. We look to you for guidance!"

Upon their sincere request, the Buddha accepted them promptly and helped shave their heads and beards. The five hundred Brahman archers then began to cultivate with their greatest efforts in accordance with the Buddha's instructions.

The Redemption of Angulimalya

In the village of Sana, north of Sravasti, there lived a prominent Brahman. Angulimalya was this Brahman's favorite disciple, because he was so obedient and respectful to him. The other disciples were jealous of him, so they spread rumors about a relationship between the young man and the Brahman's wife.

The Brahman's wife happened to actually be in love with Angulimalya. One day, when her husband was away, she tried to seduce him. Angulimalya was enraged by her attempted seduction. Knowing that such a thing was very immoral, he scolded her angrily, "You are older than I am and I respect you as my mother. This is a sacred place, please watch your behavior."

The Brahman's wife was so embarrassed that she became determined to destroy the young man's reputation. Thus she ripped her clothes, set her hair in disarray, and accused Angulimalya's of trying to rape her, saying that she preferred death. When the Brahman came home he was outraged and summoned Algulimalya. The Brahman told the young man, "I have taught you everything except the most important supernatural power. To gain this power and attain awakening, you must kill more than one hundred people and wear their fingers around your neck."

Algulimalya answered haltingly, "But, teacher, it is no minor thing to kill so many people. I would have to break the laws."

The Brahman continued to urge him, "Foolish man, don't you know that one can be purified only through killing? Don't you want to become a Brahman and live in heaven?" Angulimalya could not disobey his teacher, and he started a crazed killing spree.

When the Buddha's disciples became aware of this, they hurried to tell the Buddha. Some of his disciples were scared, yet the Buddha was calm and spoke with compassion, "What a pitiable man, I shall go liberate him."

The Buddha walked toward where Angulimalya did his killings. Someone mowing the grass by the roadside warned him, "Lord Buddha, please do not go any further, there is a killer over there."

The Buddha smiled and nodded, "Thank you for the warning, but I am here to end this killer's slaughter. Even if the whole world were against me, I would not be afraid. This is just one man I am dealing with." The Buddha then solemnly continued on, confident that he could subdue Angulimalya's insanity and teach the Dharma to him.

As soon as they met, Angulimalya was suddenly tamed by the Buddha's nobility. His knife fell from his hand, and he asked, "Where has this sage come from?"

The Buddha replied, "I am the Buddha. I now reside at Jetavana Monastery. In the future, I shall enter nirvana and abide in infinity and in the mind of all sentient beings. I felt compassion for you, so I decided to teach the Dharma to you in person. Will you follow me?

Angulimalya bowed and said, "I have frightened everybody away. Will you still accept me?"

The Buddha replied, "As long as you repent, all your wrongdoing will be washed away. The sun shines on everything, and when the dirty water meets the sea, it becomes clear. Even the great earth can absorb a pit of manure and turn it into pure water. Just repent constantly and you can be liberated."

The Buddha's compassion encompasses everyone, he never gives up hope on being able to remove someone's vices and lead them onto the correct path. His noble virtue can compare to the greatness of the sun, the ocean, and the earth.

PART TWO:

KINDNESS

The Buddha has profound loving-kindness and compassion for all sentient beings, even for those who would seek to end his life. Knowing the universal and unconditional compassion of the Buddha can help us all to be kinder, more patient, and more understanding. These stories show the incredible kindness of the Buddha, and his exhortations for all to practice kindness as well.

A Robe for Aniruddha

Aniruddha was a cousin of the Buddha who had followed the Buddha into the monastic life. One day, when the Buddha was teaching the Dharma, Aniruddha fell asleep. The Buddha scolded him for this behavior. Aniruddha knelt down, joined his palms and asked the Buddha to forgive him. He made a vow to never fall asleep again as long as he lived.

From then on, Aniruddha practiced diligently from dawn until dusk, and from dusk to dawn and never slept. The Buddha would tell him repeatedly that, while it was not good to be lazy, it was not good to go without rest either. The Buddha said, "All sentient beings depend on food to survive. If they do not eat, they cannot live. Our eyes need food too, and the food for our eyes is sleep."

Aniruddha, however insisted, "I vowed to never sleep again, I will not violate my vow."

Soon afterward, Aniruddha went blind. The blind Aniruddha experienced many inconveniences living in the sangha, especially collecting alms and sewing. But, there were many healthy and kind monks in the sangha who would help him. When they came back from collecting alms, they shared their food with all the sick monks, and thus obtaining food was not a problem for Aniruddha.

One day, Aniruddha's robe tore. He tried several times to mend it, but he could not. Eventually, his robes were reduced to rags, and he had to ask Ananda to help him mend the cloth.

When the Buddha found out that Aniruddha was unable to mend his own robe, he volunteered to help. The Buddha came to the cave where Aniruddha stayed. He told Aniruddha, "Bring your needle and thread and let me help you." Though blind, Aniruddha heard the Buddha's voice and was both touched and frightened. His eyes welled up with tears and he was speechless.

The Buddha threaded the needle and cut out a pattern. With the help of Ananda and the others, they finished three robes for Aniruddha in one day.

The Buddha is a teacher with perfect virtue and merit. When his disciple was blind he was loving and compassionate, and his disciple was respectful. This relationship between the master and student is followed everywhere in the Buddhist world. This story sets a good example for people in future times.

To Practice Kindness

One morning, Sariputra carried his alms bowl into town to collect alms. Soon after entering the town, he encountered an elderly woman who was weeping by the roadside. Sariputra approached her kindly and asked, "Madam, what troubles you?"

Tearfully, she replied, "Venerable, my house was robbed, and all my valuables were stolen."

After he returned to the monastery, Sariputra told the Buddha what happened that morning.

The Buddha took this opportunity to teach Sariputra, "A household consisting of many women and few men will be an easy target for thieves. In the same way, a monk who neglects the practice of kindness will be easy prey for demons and evil spirits. He will easily lose his spiritual commitment. Alternatively, a household that consists of many men and few women will deter thieves from eyeing its belongings. In the same way, a monk who takes up the practice of kindness every minute of his day accumulates immeasurable merit. Evil spirits and demons can find no way to afflict or harm him."

From this comparison Sariputra realized how precious it was for a person to leave home and cultivate according to the teachings. From then on, he treasured his practice even more.

The Buddha continued further, "The practice of kindness should be undertaken with a strong commitment so that one's cultivation will be strong and cannot be swayed by avarice. It is in this way that one can be free from evil and the defilements."

To Love Yourself

After King Prasenajit took refuge in the Buddha he would frequently visit the Buddha to express his thoughts and to listen to his teachings.

One day, the king came to the Buddha and said, "Lord Buddha, one day during meditation, I began to think about what kind of person truly loves himself, and what kind does not. I have come to this conclusion: If one performs unwholesome actions, speaks unwholesome words, and thinks unwholesome thoughts, then this person does not love himself. This kind of person treats himself without respect, and therefore he does not truly love himself.

"Alternatively, if one performs wholesome actions, speaks wholesome words, and thinks wholesome thoughts, then this person truly loves himself. Even if this person were to say, 'I do not love myself,' he treats himself with respect. This kind of person truly loves himself. Are my thoughts on this topic correct?"

The Buddha praised the king and said, "As you have said, if a person chooses unwholesome actions, words, and thoughts, then this person does not love himself. On the other hand, if a person chooses wholesome actions, words, and thoughts, this person is the one who truly loves himself."

The Buddha then spoke the following verse to sum up the king's thoughts:

> *To truly love oneself,*
> *One must not do what is unwholesome.*
> *For one who has bad karma,*
> *Cannot obtain harmony and happiness.*

Life Is Precious

Once, two neighboring countries were preparing to go to battle to fight for access to a certain river. The Buddha heard of the imminent war and went to see the kings of both countries to ask them why they were starting this war. After both kings had explained their situation, the Buddha said, "I know this river is useful to some of the people in your countries. However, is it not true that it is not needed by the majority of your people?"

"This is true. It is of no value to the majority of our people," both kings replied unequivocally.

The Buddha said, "When your two countries go to war, is it not true that numerous lives will be lost on the battlefield, perhaps even your own?"

"This is true. Many people will die and our own lives will be at risk," both kings agreed.

The Buddha then asked, "Is human life worth less than a river?"

"No! The lives of our people are invaluable."

"Then why is it necessary to sacrifice precious human life for a worthless river?"

After their conversations with the Buddha, the kings realized that they should settle the dispute in a peaceful manner.

The Buddha's wisdom diverted a bloody war and elucidated the duties and goals of a king.

To Show Gratitude

Once, just as night fell on the Bamboo Grove, some peculiar mournful cries could be heard off in the distance. After some time, these strange sounds disappeared. After that night a small fox could be seen following a novice monk around the Bamboo Grove. Some newly ordained monks wondered why this was, so they went to the Buddha to ask.

"Lord Buddha, lately we have seen a novice monk that is accompanied by a little fox wherever he goes. Can you tell us why?"

"Monks, that little fox was once badly hurt. The novice monk could not bear to leave it and let it be slaughtered by the other animals, so he saved him and treated his wounds. That was why you heard those mournful wails the other night, and why they suddenly stopped."

"After the little fox was well, he felt immense gratitude for what the novice monk had done for him. He was reluctant to leave the one who had saved his life, and in order to show his gratitude he always stayed close by to keep the novice monk company."

"How incredible! Even a fox knows about gratitude!"

"Exactly. Is it not amazing? Even a fox shows his gratitude. If a person does not know to be grateful and to repay a favor, what good is he? He is definitely inferior to an animal. Humans will despise him, and animals will avoid him. He is considered the poorest man of all. To be an upright person, we should be grateful for others' kindness and repay them. When repaying the kindness of others, you should repay a drop of water with a bubbling fountain. Only by doing this can you consider yourself rich."

"We now understand, Lord Buddha. What you tried to emphasize was that gratitude is the best wealth, and that by showing gratitude we can become happy and harmonious. Is this correct?"

The Buddha said, satisfied, "Monks, I am glad that you all have learned so fast."

One Kind Thought

The complete collection of Buddhist sutras embodies the teaching of Buddhism with its innumerable methods and themes. The foundation of all these teachings, however, lies in loving-kindness and compassion. It says in the sutras, "If the Dharma is separated from loving-kindness and compassion, it is the demon way." From this we can recognize the close relationship between the two, especially in Mahayana Buddhism where fulfilling the bodhisattva path is to put compassion into practice.

The Buddha once tried to illustrate the importance of loving-kindness and compassion through the story of the war between the asuras and celestial beings:

"Long ago, there once was a battle between the celestial beings and the asuras, and the asuras were winning. In their flight, Sakra-devanamindra ordered his troops to retreat to the north to the celestial palace. During their journey to the palace, the team of chariots had to traverse the woodlands of Mount Sumeru. When they reached the woodlands, amidst the undergrowth they discovered a garuda's nest with many of its young hatchlings inside. Sakra-devanamindra worried that the birds would not be safe if his chariots came trampling through, so he gave an order to the charioteers; 'Turn round, we must not harm the young birds!'

"The charioteers replied, 'The asura troops are right behind us. If we turn around now, we will be killed!' Sakra-devanamindra said, 'I would rather die by turning back than allow our chariots to run over these birds!'

"At this, the whole regiment turned south. The asuras were startled to see this and suspected their enemies' sudden change in direction to be a strategic move. The head of the asuras immediately ordered his troops to retreat to their own palace, and the whole situation was reversed."

After he finished telling the story, the Buddha admonished his disciples, "Sakra-devanamindra's one kind thought lead to the defeat of the asuras. You who have joined the sangha must foster kindness within yourselves in order to be victorious over the armies of greed, anger, and ignorance. Keep this in mind and remember it well."

It says in the sutras that bodhisattvas develop great compassion to liberate all sentient beings. Through great compassion they nurture the seeds of bodhi within, which allow them to become Buddhas. If bodhisattvas witness the suffering of sentient beings without initiating loving-kindness and compassion and without resolving to realize the Way in order to relieve their torment, then they will not attain awakening. Compassion is the prerequisite for the bodhisattva's attainment of Buddhahood.

The Four Actions of The Wise

One day when the Buddha was teaching at Jetavana Monastery, he told his disciples, "There are four actions the wise follow, while the foolish do not care to know:

"First, a wise person respects his parents and teachers and makes offerings to them. He does not let them live in poverty.

"Second, a wise person is kind to others, and cares for everyone. He takes care of his property and does not kill living things.

"Third, a wise person practices generosity. He always helps those who are poor or in need.

"Fourth, a wise person abides by the Dharma and practices diligently. If you practice these four actions you will soon reach the path of purity."

The Buddha then told his disciples, "There are two other practices you should all learn. Wether you are in public or in private, you should observe your mind. Do not stay in the fog of delusion— stay alert. In private, you should focus on contemplation and meditation. In public, you should learn, teach, and discuss the breadth of the Dharma.

"There are two kinds of generosity you should practice. The first is to offer delicious food to others. This is called the offering of food. You can also teach the Dharma to others. This is called the offering of Dharma. Of all the possible offerings, the offering of Dharma is the best. You should consider teaching the Dharma to be your responsibility. This is called true practice."

After the Buddha had spoken, all his disciples gladly followed his teachings.

Devadatta Falls Ill

Time and again, Devadatta opposed the Buddha, plotting against him, and even made attempts on his life several times. One day, Devadatta fell ill. When all the doctors failed to find a cure, the Buddha went to see him.

One follower asked the Buddha, "Lord Buddha, why do you still want to help Devadatta who has made so many vicious attempts to frame and even kill you?"

The Buddha replied, "If we only befriend some people and treat others as our enemies, we are not being reasonable. All sentient beings are equal. Everyone wants to have happiness; nobody likes sickness or sorrow. We must have compassion towards everyone."

The Buddha went to the bedside of Devadatta and said, "If I truly love and care for my cousin Devadatta, who has frequently attempted to harm me, as much as I do my only son Rahula, may my cousin's illness be immediately cured." After he had said this, Devadatta was indeed cured without any medication.

The Buddha turned around and addressed his followers,

"Everyone must know that in my eyes, I see all beings just as I see my only son Rahula. I love them all without any exception."

The Buddha had mentioned in the sutras that Devadatta had been a good Dharma friend for him. People who are bad and stubborn are the ones who require the most compassion to liberate, as demonstrated by the Buddha's love and care towards the seriously ill. As the Buddha treats all beings as if they were his own son Rahula, we know that his love for all sentient beings is pure and kind.

Modesty and Humility

One year during the rains retreat the Buddha resided at Jetavana Monastery while his disciples spent the retreat elsewhere. When the ninety-day retreat period was over, all his disciples returned to Jetavana Monastery to greet the Buddha and listen to his teaching.

The Buddha had not seen his followers during this long retreat period and was pleased to see them return. He waved hello to them, and humbly inquired about the adequacy of food and offerings while on retreat in isolated areas. This modest and caring attitude of someone with such incomparable merit greatly impressed Ananda, who was always by the Buddha's side and at his service. Deeply perplexed, he asked the Buddha, "Lord Buddha, your birth into this world has been most extraordinary, merit and wisdom like yours is rare. Why do you still feel it is necessary to greet the monks with such humility?" In response the Buddha recounted to Ananda the incident that brought about his humility:

Long ago, there was a country called Varanasi. In Varanasi there lived a man who was thrifty by nature and loved to hoard gold. What he saved from his frugal spending practices he used to buy gold, which was stored in jars. He had these jars buried in an underground cave below his home.

As the years went by, he gradually saved up seven jars of gold. When the man died, his deep love for this gold resulted in his being reborn as a venomous snake to guard the jars. As the years passed, his house became dilapidated and deserted. However, he was reborn as a snake lifetime after lifetime to guard the gold he so strongly coveted. After thousands of years had gone by, the snake suddenly felt tired of being a snake. He realized that unless he ceased his obsession with the gold, he would keep returning as a snake. Thus he resolved to give away the gold in order to gain some merit.

Leaving the jars of gold, the snake came to the roadside and hid among the thick grass, awaiting a kind-hearted person to help him realize his wish. Seeing a farmer approaching, he called out to him. The farmer heard the snake's sound but could not see who was calling, so he continued walking. Eventually, the snake had to reveal himself to the farmer to ask for his help. Seeing that the snake did not mean any harm, the farmer agreed to help him. The snake lead him to the cave where the gold was stored, and requested that the gold be used for food offerings to the monastics in a Buddhist temple. The snake also asked to be taken along so that he could listen to the Dharma.

On the day of the food offering, the farmer carried the snake in a basket to the temple. Along the way, a man came up to greet the farmer, who would not respond even after repeated greetings. The snake was very annoyed at the farmer's behavior and thought, "Why is this farmer so impolite? Why did he not respond to such friendly questions?" Angrily, the snake repeatedly thought of harming the farmer. In the end, the snake decided to be patient, as he thought it would be ungrateful to hurt someone who had done him a favor. However, when they came to an open area, the snake asked to be released, and it proceeded to reprimand the farmer for being arrogant and unreasonable. The farmer was filled with shame and remorse; a sense of humility arose in his mind, and he vowed to be kind to all beings from that day forward.

When they finally reached the temple, the farmer placed the snake in front of the monks. When the offering began, the snake ordered the farmer to offer incense accordingly, while he watched the recipients with absolute faith. After the monks had circled around the pagoda, the farmer prepared water for the monks to cleanse their hands in readiness for the food offering. During this whole process, the snake was patient and respectful. After the meal, the snake took refuge with the monks, who gave him a teaching on generosity, upholding the precepts, patience and diligence. The snake joyfully offered all his gold, and the merit thus attained enabled him to be reborn in the heaven of the thirty-three when he died.

The Buddha told Ananda, "In the past, I was the farmer and the snake is now the one who is the foremost in wisdom among my disciples, Sariputra. I was the one who developed great remorse when rebuked by the snake. After many kalpas, I have not altered my vow nor lessened my determination to act with modesty and humility toward all living beings."

All the disciples felt great happiness after listening to the story, and they gladly followed the Buddha's teachings.

The Three Levels of Filial Piety

Uttara was a fine young man with good moral conduct who was especially commended by his peers for his respectful behavior towards the elderly and his filial piety towards his parents.

One day, Uttara went to the Monastery to hear the Buddha's teachings. When the Buddha was referring to the importance of cultivating merit, Uttara asked the Buddha, "Lord Buddha, I have continuously served my parents in accordance with the Dharma so that they could be comfortable and happy. Lord Buddha, will I receive any merit because of this?"

The Buddha replied, "Anyone who does so will receive great merit. However, one's practice of filial piety can be classified into three different levels."

"Oh, there are different levels of filial piety?" Uttara asked.

"Yes, there are three different levels. The first level is to provide for one's parents abundant food and material supplies while they are alive and affording them a decent burial at their death. This is the smallest level of filial piety.

"The second level is to build a successful career which brings honor to the family name in addition to providing material offerings. In this way one's parents can share in one's glory. This is the moderate level of filial piety.

"The third level is to introduce and guide one's parents towards the Dharma such that they can relieve the suffering of future rebirth. This is the greatest level of filial piety. Uttara, which level would you like to achieve?"

Uttara bowed before the Buddha in respect, "Lord Buddha, I now understand that only providing good material provisions for my parents is not enough. From now on, I will aim for the greatest level of filial piety with all of my effort."

Being filial to our parents and providing for them is the proper behavior of every son and daughter. Even someone with such perfect merit and wisdom as the Buddha personally carried his father's coffin and went to the heaven of the thirty-three to teach the Dharma to his mother. Thus, the Buddha established the ideal example of filial piety for future Buddhists. As followers of the Buddha, we should fulfill our filial responsibilities towards our parents as the first step in our study of Buddhism.

PART THREE:

KARMA

The Buddha taught the law of karma: that everything in this world arises due to causes and conditions, and that everything we do has an effect upon ourselves, those around us, and the world. He taught that every action, every word, and every thought plants a seed that will one day bear fruit.

The Buddha did not teach us the law of karma so that we could be trapped in our fate, but instead to set us free. Karma is what allows us to take control of our lives and change our destiny. These stories show the workings of karma— the lives affected by the actions of the past, as well as the future that is being built each moment.

The Yellow Plum Tree

There once was a wealthy Brahman elder whose only son had just turned twenty and had been married for less than seven days. The young couple got along harmoniously and treated each other with respect.

One beautiful spring day, the couple took a walk in the backyard to see the blooming flowers. The plum tree in the garden was covered with blossoms. The wife thought to herself, "I would love to have some of these fresh flowers. Who can pick some for me?" The husband guessed his wife's thoughts and immediately climbed up the tree to pick a flower for her. Once he was hanging in the branches of the plum tree, he then saw more pretty flowers on the thinner branches. He could not resist temptation and climbed toward the small branches. All of a sudden, the branch broke and the husband fell to the ground and died immediately.

When the family heard the wife's cry, they ran out to the garden. The father went to his son's dead body, crying his heart out. Visiting friends and relatives all felt great sorrow.

Everyone who heard the news was stricken with grief, and even those who only heard the bad news were very saddened. After the funeral, the family could not stop crying. The parents blamed the gods for not protecting their son. The Buddha sensed their ignorance and decided to visit the family in person. When they saw the Buddha, they all cried, and bowed before him. They told the Buddha what had happened.

The Buddha told the elder, "Cry no more and listen to me. Everything in this world is impermanent. Whenever there is life, there will be death. Even if you killed yourself, you cannot revive your son. Fortune and misfortune cannot be separated from each other. There are three groups crying over the death of this child. Whose son is he and who are his parents?" The Buddha shared with them this verse:

"Human life is like a blooming flower or a ripened fruit.
It is destined to fall to the ground.

There is only suffering after birth.
Who on the earth is immune to death?"

The conception of new life comes from the passion of love.
Human life runs like a stream through day and night.

This human body dies,
and the spirit is formless.

One future rebirth is formed
From the karma of previous lives.

Life after life, through prolonged love and affection,
Ignorantly believing they are enjoying life

The cycle of rebirth continues,
And the spirit goes on.

After hearing the verse, the father became awakened and forgot his suffering. He knelt down and asked the Buddha, "What had my son done in the past to cause such an early death?"

The Buddha told the father, "Once there was a little boy who went to play under a tree with a bow and arrow. There were three other children playing under the same tree. When the boy saw a sparrow in the tree, he was eager to shoot it down. The other children were also excited and encouraged him, 'If you can shoot down the sparrow, you are a true hero.' The child was flattered, aimed at the sparrow, and shot. The boys cheered and applauded with great joy, and then gladly went home.

"In later lives, these four kids often encountered each other over many lifetimes and felt the karmic effects of their wrongdoing. One of them was born in heaven to enjoy the fortune he had accumulated in the past. The second one was born in the sea to become a dragon king. The third one is you, born as a human being. The child who killed the sparrow was once born in heaven, to be the son of a god. After that life, he was born in the human realm and became your son. Because of this past cause, he fell out of the tree and died. He will now be born in the sea as the son of the dragon king. After he is born, he will be eaten by a garuda, who was the sparrow in its past life.

Life and death, as well as cause and effect, are complicated and hard to explain. Because you three encouraged the boy to shoot the sparrow and praised him afterwards, you will experience the negative karmic effect in heaven, in the sea, and in the human realm."

The Buddha then spoke another verse:

> "Our mind created the existence of the three realms,"
> Some realms are fortunate and others are unfortunate.
> Whichever realm you are in, karma has sent you there.
> Your actions in previous lives determine the formation of
> this life.

Depending on the seeds you plant, karma follows like a shadow."

The father was relieved after hearing the Buddha's teachings. The whole family took refuge in the Buddha and observed the five precepts.

The Brahman Blocks the Way

One day, while the Buddha was living at Jetavana Monastery in Sravasti, he led his monks into the city to collect alms. When they entered an alley, they encountered a Brahman who blocked their way. He drew a line on the ground and would not let the Buddha pass. The Brahman rudely shouted, "Give me five hundred gold coins, or you must stay there." When the Buddha and his disciples heard his demand, they could do nothing but stand there quietly.

The news of the Brahman's bullying went all the way to King Bimbisara and King Prasenajit. They immediately sent servants to bring jewels to the Brahman. However, the Brahman would not accept their jewels. Later, when the elder Sudatta heard that the Buddha was held up by the Brahman, he immediately sent five hundred coins and, to everyone's surprise, the Brahman took the gold and let the Buddha pass.

The monks were amazed. They asked the Buddha, "Lord Buddha, what have you done to this Brahman and why did he stop us?"

The Buddha answered, "A long time ago, there was a prince in Varanasi named Sujata. One day, Prince Sujata and his friends went out to play and met a person who was gambling with the prime minister's son. They both bet five hundred gold pieces. The prime minister's son lost but, because of his position, he simply refused to pay. At that time, the prince told the minister, 'If the prime minister's son does not want to pay, I will pay for him.' From then on, across infinite lifetimes, this person has been after me."

The Buddha continued, "That prince was me in a previous life. The prime minister's son was the elder Sudatta. His opponent was the Brahman we met today. Therefore, if you owe a debt, you should not lie or refuse to pay it back. Even if you have attained Buddhahood, you still cannot avoid the effects of unwholesome karma."

After the disciples heard the law of cause and effect, they all became more cautious and followed the Buddha's teachings.

Previous and future lives are dependent upon each other. The effect is embedded in the cause and the cause is embedded in the effect. Cause and effect interlock like links in a chain from one life to the next. One's karma does not disappear after death. It will follow you until it reaches fruition.

We Reap What We Sow

There once was a young man who was a devoted follower of a non-Buddhist sect. Whenever he encountered difficulty, he would worship the gods and ask them to protect him. In recent years, he had become weak and was often ill. He worshipped the gods even more diligently, but his health did not improve.

At that time, he heard that the Buddha was a good teacher who could help people understand the true nature of things, so he went to see the Buddha and asked him to show him how to maintain good health.

The Buddha pointed out to the young man a group of farmers, "Look at these farmers. They work diligently in the spring to sow seeds and plow the ground. That's why they get a good harvest in the fall. If they just pray everyday and do not sow, will they be able to harvest their crops in the fall?"

"No," the young man answered, "If they do not sow the seeds, it does not matter how much they pray to the gods, the wasted land will grow nothing."

"Correct. In the same way, praying to the gods is not going to relieve your suffering, either. If you take care of your body, pay attention to your nutrition, have the proper amount of exercise and rest, and maintain proper balance in your physical and mental activities, then you will have good health. It is just like farming. If you sow the seeds and plow the ground, the seeds will sprout."

The young man listened to the Buddha's teachings, his mind began to clear, and he attained awakening. Immediately, he decided to take refugee in the Buddha and became a lay Buddhist follower.

Everything in this world follows the Law of Cause and Effect. Health has its causes. Fortune has its causes. If you want to have a good harvest in the fall, you must sow the seeds and plow the ground in the spring. Nothing can be gained without planting seeds. If you plant seeds and wait patiently, you will gain the fruit.

Ordaining A Drunkard

One day, while the Buddha was at Jetavana Monastery, a
drunken Brahman came to him and requested to be ordained as
a monk. The Buddha ordered Ananda to shave his head and
clothe him in monastic robes. However, when the man became
sober again and found himself dressed as a monk, he fled in
terror.

A group of monks came over and asked the Buddha, "Why
did you allow a drunkard to become a monk?"

The Buddha replied, "In the countless kalpas of the past, this
Brahman has never had the thought of leaving home to become
a monk. Today, due to his drunkenness, his mind briefly focused
on awakening. Although it was not his original intention, the
good karma he has planted today will enable him to become a
monk and attain awakening in the future. How can I afford to let
this opportunity slip by?"

*To continuously nurture the bodhi mind requires great merit
and virtue. Although the Buddha can only liberate those beings
with the appropriate causes and conditions, he will not forget to
plant the seeds of the awakening in all beings.*

Like a Lost Goat

In Rajagrha there lived a particularly cruel and foolish man. He did not obey his parents, he bullied the meek, and paid no respect to his elders. As time went on, his wealth dwindled. Since he believed in the fire god, the sun god, and the moon god, he asked them to bless him with good fortune on earth and in heaven. For a long period of time, he spent large amounts of money worshipping the gods but did not receive any merit from them.

He heard that the Buddha was currently teaching the Dharma in Sravasti, so he left his home and went to the Jatavana Monastery to pay homage to the Buddha. He asked the Buddha to teach him how to become wealthy, "Lord, Buddha, I am a fool. I did not know about the Buddha, the Dharma, and the Sangha. I spent nine years worshipping the fire god, sun god, and moon god but did not receive any merit from them. I now looked haggard and will soon die. I came a great distance to see you, please give me some advice."

The Buddha told him, "You believe in evil spirits. Even if your prayers are as lofty as Mt. Sumeru, your bad karma is as deep as the sea. Since you sacrifice animals to worship the gods, you have only decreased your merit and virtue. Even if you spent a hundred kalpas diligently killing pigs, oxen, and goats to worship your gods, you would not receive any merit. The unwholesome karma from those acts could stretch as high as Mt. Sumeru.

"You have wasted time and money for many years. You are like a lost goat. You do not know to obey your parents. You oppress good people and do not respect your teachers and elders.

You are prideful and lazy. You consider others beneath you. You are burning with greed, anger and ignorance. These three things are poisonous and only make your karma worse and worse.

"If you change your ways and start respecting the wise, and taking care of your elders, start performing good deeds, cultivate your character, and purify your mind and body, disaster and misfortune will never befall you. You will accumulate four kinds of merit. What are these four? First of all, you will have a dignified appearance. Secondly, you will have a strong body. Third, you will enjoy good health and tranquility. Fourth, you will enjoy longevity, and no misfortune will ever happen to you. If you can follow my teaching faithfully, you will receive these four kinds of merit."

Then the Buddha spoke to him in verse:

> *"Worshipping the gods and praying for good fortune, will not achieve anything.*
> *It is better to respect the wise, have proper conduct, and to respect elders.*
> *In this way, you accumulate four kinds of merit.*
> *Your body will be strong, and you will enjoy longevity and tranquility."*

The foolish man listened to the Buddha's verse and was deeply touched. He told the Buddha, "I am so ignorant. I have created bad karma for the past nine years. Fortunately, due to your teaching, I have now eliminated my ignorance. Please allow me to join the sangha and follow you." The Buddha compassionately accepted him as a disciple.

One must follow the correct path in pursuing fortune. Worshipping the gods and killing living beings in exchange for good fortune, is like trying to go fishing in a tree. This leads one farther and farther away from the right path.

Oppressed by the Brahmans

When the Brahmans and the followers of the other wandering sects in Sravasti saw how quickly the Buddha's influence was growing, they became inflamed with jealousy. They would not be satisfied until they could somehow harm the Buddha.

After careful scheming, they hired a young girl to do their bidding. They asked her to put on beautiful clothes, hold fresh flowers in her hands, and follow the Buddha's devotees to Jetavana Monastery. That night, she hid near the monastery. The next morning, as the villagers began to arrive at Jetavana to pay homage to the Buddha they greeted the girl, who told them she had spent the night at Jetavana Monastery.

Seven or eight months later, she started tying a small wooden basin to her stomach. One day, as the Buddha was teaching the Dharma, the young girl joined the audience, dressed like a pregnant woman. All of a sudden, she stood up in public and scolded the Buddha, "Since you can speak so eloquently, let me ask you this question: you and I had an intimate relationship, why haven't you built a house for me to deliver our baby? You abandoned and ignored me! You are a cold-blooded, unfaithful person!"

After she made such a proclaimation, even those truly devoted in the audience lost their composure. But, the Buddha did not move. He sat solemnly in his seat with his eyes closed. The wooden basin fell with a flop to the ground. The vicious scheme of the Brahmans was exposed. Ashamed, the girl ran out of the monastery. The Buddha then calmly resumed teaching.

Even after their malicious scheme was exposed, the Brahmans still refused to come to their senses. This time they ordered a young Brahman girl to frequently visit Jetavana Monastery. Several days later, the Brahmans hired assassins to kill the girl. As she walked toward the monastery, they murdered her and buried the body in refuse heap near the monastery. The next day, the Brahmans reported the missing person to the city. After a careful search, they found her body near Jetavana.

The Brahmans spread the word throughout the community: the murdered girl had an affair with someone within Jetavana Monastery, and her unfortunate death must have been caused by her tangled love affair. The Buddha's followers knew this must be the scheme of the Brahmans, but how could they prove the sangha was innocent? Everyone was very worried, so they reported the story to the Buddha. After the Buddha listened to them, he asked a monk to go out to the street and tell the public, "Killing is brutal and unforgivable thing. If one kills a person and then incriminates others for the killing, he has committed both the crimes of killing and lying. Sooner or later, he will feel the karmic effect of his treacherous actions."

The sangha endured this unfortunate slander. However, those who believed in the Buddha knew his sangha was innocent. King Prasenajit in Sravasti was a devoted follower of the Buddha and lived in accordance with the Dharma. He did not doubt the sangha's innocence. Since the Buddha did not give any indication, the king ordered his officials to solve the case quickly and to reveal the truth to the public.

The Buddha said "No matter if it is good or bad, your karma will follow you like a shadow." Soon after the assassins received their reward from the Brahmans and went drinking and playing games at a tavern. They began to fight over how to split their reward money and were arrested. They confessed all they had done and who hired them. King Prasenajit ordered the officials to arrest the Brahmans for their crimes. The truth was announced to the public and the Brahmans were exiled. The Buddha's reputation shone like the sun and the moon. All the people of Sravasti rushed to take refuge in and support the Buddha.

If there is no darkness, light cannot manifest. If there is no evil, one cannot see virtue. The spreading of the Dharma is propelled by the evil and crime in the world.

The Buddha Smiles

The Buddha would often journey from place to place to teach the Dharma. One day, while passing by a village, he saw an old man selling fish in the market. The old man cried, "Why does heaven treat me with such cruelty? What crime has my son committed that he deserved to die so young? If he were still alive today, I would not have to work so hard." When the Buddha saw the old man crying sadly, he smiled. Soon after, the Buddha saw a fat pig walking along the street, its body full of urine and feces. The Buddha smiled again.

Ananda was surprised. He went in front of the Buddha and respectfully asked, "Lord Buddha, why did you smile at these misfortunes today? You would not smile for no reason. There must be a reason. Please, explain the reason to me, so that I may understand."

"Ananda, that is a very good question. There are three reasons why I smiled today. First, I wanted to use the ignorance of this old man's behavior as an example to teach people. That old man fishes everyday. He has taken many lives without sympathy. Yet, when his son is dead, he cries and complains that heaven took his son's life. This is very foolish behavior.

"Second, the old man was an emperor in his past life. Even though this emperor had accumulated great merit, he was a proud and stubborn person. As a result, he was reborn as a fisherman in this life and relies on fishing to make a living.

"Third, the fish in the bamboo basket lived in the no thought heaven in its past life. Beings who live in that heaven, have an average lifespan of 8,040 million kalpas. Yet, he was attached to emptiness. He did not realize that even emptiness is empty. After his merit was extinguished, he was reborn as a fish and was caught by the old man."

"Lord Buddha, even if one becomes an emperor with high power and prestige, one still cannot escape the effects of one's karma?" Ananda asked.

"Ananda," replied the Buddha, "misfortune and fortune are impermanent. When a person is in a high position, enjoying honor and fortune, he should spread his fortune to others in order to avoid misfortune. If a person boasts about his own honor and fortune and does whatever unwholesome acts he desires, when his fortune is used up, he will suffer the effects of that unwholesome karma.

"The effects of your karma will follow you, just as a shadow follows a form or an echo follows a sound. This law of nature applies to both the noble and the humble.

"In a past life, I practiced in accordance with the Dharma while my neighbors worshiped gods and ghosts and committed many crimes. Unfortunate things happened to them like an echo following a sound. I used to go to the temple on observance days to listen to the Dharma and to cultivate my virtue. I eventually attained Buddhahood. I am now the one honored by the three realms of existence.

"Since my neighbor was immersed in worshipping ghosts, killing, intoxication, and adultery, he remains in the lower realms of rebirth. I have attained Buddhahood, while he is still a dirty pig. Ananda, since I have diligently listened to the Dharma and learned from my companions in the holy life, I have attained these wonderful bodily features."

After the Buddha spoke, he looked at his audience sympathetically.

Power cannot change the Law of Cause and Effect. Gods and ghosts cannot change it. Heaven cannot change it. This law governs everything in the universe. The consequences of wholesome conduct or unwholesome conduct follows us like a shadow until it manifests itself. Cause and effect follow each other in our past, present and future lives. If we waste this life, we will regret it forever. If we continue to accumulate merit, we will obtain wisdom and good fortune in this life and in future lives as well.

Cultivating Merit Again

In Sravasti, there was an old monk with very poor eyesight. One day, he tore his robe. He was trying to piece it together but was unable to pull the thread through the eye of the needle. Greatly troubled by this, he pleaded, "Who would like to perform a good deed and accumulate merit? Come and help me thread the needle, please."

When the Buddha heard this, he immediately went over to help him thread the needle. The old monk recognized the Buddha's voice, and asked, "Lord Buddha, through countless kalpas you have practiced loving kindness and done many good deeds for the benefit of others. Your merit, virtue and discipline have been perfected. Why do you need to come here to help me thread the needle to accumulate more merit?"

The Buddha said to the old monk, "I never lost the habit of doing kind deeds— that is why I have come to help you. One should never stop making merit."

"Do not do something wrong just because it seems trivial; do not neglect to do something good just because it seems small." Even the Buddha, who is awakened and has perfect virtue, does not overlook a small opportunity to act with kindness. As Buddhists we must remember that in order to be virtuous we should start by accumulating small virtues. Without doing so, we cannot become virtuous. We should practice wholesome deeds in our daily lives.

Virtuous Light

King Prasenajit had a daughter named "Virtuous Light." She was intelligent, clever, and pretty. She was loved by her parents and respected by everyone in the palace.

One day, the king said to the princess, "My daughter, you have grown up in a royal family surrounded by luxuries and you are respected by all. It is I who grant you your glory and wealth."

Virtuous Light was a follower of the Buddha and understood the law of cause and effect, so she answered her father, "Your Majesty, one's fortune and prosperity are due to one's karma and are not granted by others. What I have in my life comes from the power of good deeds accumulated in past lives, and does not come from you."

The king stated his belief to her three times, but she responded in the same way each time. He was enraged by his daughter's disobedience and said, "Today we will find out how great your karma is, since that is what you believe in."

Thus the king ordered his ministers to find the poorest beggar in the city. The king then forced his daughter to marry the man. After conducting their wedding, the king said "As long as you have your karma, you should enjoy wealth and esteem without me. From now on, I will see if what you have said is true."

Virtuous Light responded firmly, "Surely I will still see the effects of my good karma." Then she left the palace with the poor man.

Virtuous Light asked her husband, "Do you have parents?"

The poor man answered, "When my father was alive, he was the most respected elder in Sravasti. However, after my parents passed away, I had nobody to rely on and was forced to beg for a living."

"Do you still remember where your old home is?" Virtuous Light asked.

"I certainly know where it is, but the house has long fallen into ruin. There is nothing there but an empty lot."

Virtuous Light and her husband decided to return to the deserted lost. Virtuous Light walked around the empty lot, and everywhere she stepped the earth gave way and revealed countless treasures. With these treasures, Virtuous Light built a magnificent palace and hired many servants, maids, and entertainers.

One day, the king thought of his daughter and wondered how she was doing. An attendant told him, "Virtuous Light owns a palace and her wealth is no less than yours!"

The king finally believed the incredible power of karma, "As the Buddha says, one truly experiences gain and loss based on one's former wholesome and unwholesome action."

The king then went to where the Buddha was residing to ask him a question, "What good deeds has my daughter done in her former lives to allow her to be born in a royal family with splendor all around her?"

The Buddha answered, "Ninety-one kalpas ago there was a Buddha named Vipasyin. The king at that time built a stupa to make offerings to the Buddha's relics after Vipasyin entered parinirvana. The king's first wife put a crown on the head of the Buddha statue and placed pearls on both sides of the door. Suddenly, bright light shone all around and the wife made a vow, 'May my future life be filled with shinning lights, bestowed with wealth and esteem, instead of falling into the three lower realms or the eight difficult conditions.' This first wife was the present Virtuous Light.

"Again in the age of Kasyapa Buddha, there was a lady who wished to offer some food to the Buddha and his four major disciples. When the lady's husband tried to stop her, she persuaded him by saying, 'Please do not stop me! All the merit and virtue I enjoy now is the result of making offerings to the Tathagatas of the past.' The husband then allowed her to proceed with her offering. That husband is now Virtuous Light's present husband and that lady is Virtuous Light. Since that husband tried to stop the offering, he had to endure poverty in this life. He followed the lady's advice afterwards, so he has regained prosperity in this life due to Virtuous Light. It is true that wholesome and unwholesome actions bring corresponding results."

After hearing the Buddha's words, the king deeply understood the importance of good deeds. He left joyfully and ended his arrogance.

When karmic effects reach fruition, they rush in like a raging river and cannot be stopped. What seems to be impending wealth can slip away when one does not have sufficient good causes and conditions. Gods do not have the power to decide whether or not one enjoys good fortune and a long life. An outside person cannot decide that, either. Even family members and relatives can only help the realization of one's karmic results.

How can one obtain well-being and a long life? It depends on the causes and effects planted by ourselves. Our present good fortune is due to accumulated merit from the past while our future blessings depend on our current actions. We should treasure our wholesome actions, as well as treasuring our current good fortune and cultivate for our future lives. Enjoying present blessings is like lighting an oil lamp: the fuel will soon be consumed. Cultivating for future well-being is like refilling the lamp's oil so that the flame will continue to shine. We should cherish our present good causes and conditions and make an effort to plant future ones so that we will be able to enjoy future happiness.

Protecting the Dharma

One day, King Bimbisara visited the Bamboo Grove in Rajagrha. He joined the bodhisattvas and monastics in listening to the Buddha give a teaching on taking refuge in the Triple Gem, the merit of devotion, and making offerings.

King Bimbisara respectfully said to the Buddha, "Lord Buddha, these earnest devotees are joyful because of your teachings, and have offered land and buildings to the sangha. If someone were to seize this property and loot the donations given by the devotees, what would be the karmic effect of such an action?"

The Buddha replied, "Your Majesty, you need not ask about the karmic effect of committing such violations."

King Bimbisara was afraid that in the future people would not have faith in the Dharma and the Law of Cause and Effect, and that they may not understand the seriousness of robbing the sangha. He again asked the Buddha to expound on the karmic effect of stealing the property of the sangha.

The Buddha said, "The karmic effect of robbing others of what is given as alms is extremely serious."

King Bimbisara persisted, "Lord Buddha, please kindly teach us so that the people of the future who sincerely believe in the

Dharma and understand the Law of Cause and Effect will be able to maintain the proper discipline, purify their body and mind to support the Triple Gem, and be able to protect the monastics who practice in accordance with the Dharma from aggression and prosecution."

The Buddha nodded and said, "Your Majesty, you have spoken well. If people in the future do not have faith in the Dharma and the Law of Cause and Effect and thus invade temples and steal the money donated by devotees, they will face twenty different negative karmic effects: All good celestial beings will leave them. Their infamy will be known to all. They will be despised and rejected by family and friends. They will make devious friends and associate with hateful people. They will lose all their wealth. They will become mentally deranged and retarded, and also troubled and irritable. They will become crippled. They will not sleep well. They will often suffer from hunger and thirst. When they do eat it will be like ingesting poison. Their loved ones will desert them. They will argue frequently with their colleagues. No one will trust them. Their secrets will be revealed by their relatives and friends. All their wealth will be destroyed by fire, flood, the government, robbers or wayward children. They will suffer from serious illness with nobody to care for them. Their daily life will be full of obstacles. They will be physically weak and emaciated. They will suffer constant anguish. They will also live in filth until they die.

"Your Majesty, these are the twenty karmic effects that will befall such foolish people. After death they will be reborn in hell, the realm of hungry ghosts, or as an animal. There they will endure all sorts of suffering within the cycle of rebirth in these realms. After many kalpas, the karma from their crimes will gradually dissipate, and they then will be reborn as human beings with defective sense organs, and they will have such ghastly appearances that no one will want to look at them.

"Why are these karmic effects so severe? Because monastics cultivate and practice according to the Dharma for the benefit of all sentient beings. If ignorant criminals should seize others' donations for their own benefit, they will bear these severe karmic effects as punishment."

King Bimbisara, with tears steaming down his face, said, "Lord Buddha, I would rather suffer the pain of hell than invade and loot the temples."

The Buddha replied, "Those in positions of power must protect the monastics who practice in accordance with the Dharma, and not allow wicked people to harm those on the right path."

King Bimbisara further asked, "What would befall a ruler of a country if he cannot stop the looting?"

The Buddha replied, "When one possesses the merit and virtue of a sravaka or pratyekabuddha, are not the virtues of this person tremendous?"

"Yes, Lord Buddha. This person's virtues are immeasurable."

"If someone amputates the limbs of such a meritorious sage, what would be the result of this person's crime?"

The king wept uncontrollably, "Lord Buddha, this person's negative karma would be infinite! The negative karmic effect of harming a virtuous person is endless. One who harms a sage with perfect virtue will certainly receive an even more severe punishment."

The Buddha said, "If the rulers of the future cannot punish these wicked people according to the law established to protect temple property, they will experience unlimited negative karmic effects."

King Bimbisara replied rather helplessly, "Lord Buddha, it is a very difficult task for a ruler to always act for the benefit of his country and people. The ruler must constantly be alert so that he will leave no opportunity for wicked people to harm others. Any carelessness will bring him infinite suffering in the future. If a king can overcome all adversity and protect the esteemed monastics from persecution, he will attain great merit."

The Buddha said compassionately, "Yes, Your Majesty, the resulting merit and virtue would be limitless."

After listening to the Buddha's earnest advice, King Bimbisara nodded and promised, "Lord Buddha, I shall follow your teachings and support and protect the Dharma."

To have loving-kindness and compassion means to selflessly serve and help others through wisdom; without the expectation of reward. This is a great vow to benefit others. The Buddha's earnest instructions for rulers to care for the people of present and future generations is an act of immense and unlimited compassion for all beings.

Seeing Serpents

Once, while the Buddha and Ananda were out collecting alms, they encountered a pile of gold by the roadside. The Buddha said, "Ananda, do you see those serpents?"

Ananda looked at the pile of gold and agreed, "Yes, Lord Buddha, I see them. They are serpents all right." They talked as they continued their journey.

At the same time a father and son who were working in the field overheard the Buddha and Ananda's conversation and rushed to the roadside to see the serpents. Yet, to their great amazement, they found a pile of gold. "What serpents were they talking about? It's gold! How foolish the Buddha and Ananda must be!" The father and son were overjoyed and brought the gold back to their home. Though they formerly lived the lives of destitute farmers, they were now millionaires.

Since the farmers no longer had to work so hard to plow the fields they instead lived comfortable and happy lives. One of their neighbors who was jealous of their sudden fortune, was eager to find out how they became so wealthy.

He started to investigate what had brought about their extravagance. Before long he found out from a local boy that the farmers had become rich by finding gold on the roadside. He immediately reported this to the king. At that time, common citizens were not allowed to possess gold. The pile of gold had actually been stolen from the national treasury. Naturally, the father and son became the prime suspects. Soon they were captured and thrown in prison.

As the two lie in prison with their bodies sorely beaten and covered with wounds, they recall the conversation between the Buddha and Ananda. The father murmured, "Ananda, do you see those serpents?" The son looked at his father, "Yes, Lord Buddha, I see them. They are serpents all right."

The prison warden happened to overhear their conversation and felt the whole thing was suspicious and reported exactly what he heard to the king. The king then instructed someone to more deeply investigate the case and the farmers were finally released. As the king released them, he said the following words:

"The great and compassionate Buddha called the gold serpents, for he was warning people to stay away from danger. You two did not believe in his words and were punished for your greed and wrongdoing. Since you now remember the Buddha's warning with regret, your sentence can be voided."

The Dharma teaches us to remove worldly desire because it is only through going beyond the worldly that we can be free from troubles. Yet some people misinterpret the Dharma and think that it scorns money such that good Buddhists should be reluctant to speak of money or even advocate poverty. This is absurd. Why is it not possible to become prosperous while staying on the right path?

The Dharma is not good or bad, good and bad are just phenomena. Money itself is neither good nor bad, it is how it is spent that determines how it is classified. If money is used improperly, it is like a serpent. However, it if it used properly it is a means to benefit the propagation of the Dharma. A good Buddhist should not despise money that is acquired through proper ways. Instead, it should be viewed as a pure means by which to spread the Dharma. We must be aware that while our wealth is due to our karma, it is only if we spend it correctly that it can be called true wisdom.

PART FOUR:

THE BUDDHA

While the Dharma is a treasury of teachings that help us live a better life, there is also much to be learned from looking beyond what the Buddha said and into the Buddha's character. The Buddha did not teach us only with his words, but through his manner, his compassion, and his life. He was not only a perfect teacher, but he was the perfect living example of his teachings in everything he did. These stories show us the Buddha's life, and let us learn from that example.

Are You Human?

One of the thirty-two marks of excellence possessed by a Buddha is the sign of a thousand-spoked wheel on the sole of each foot. This sign, as well as the thirty-one others are not characteristics that one is simply born with, but the results of ninety-one great kalpas of spiritual practice.

One day, a Brahman took a close look at the footprints of the Buddha. In them, he saw the thousand-spoked wheel sign. Greatly surprised, he thought, "In my whole life, I have never seen a thousand-spoked wheel as dignified as these. Is the Buddha not human? Is he some kind of celestial being? I must follow these footprints and find out the truth."

With great expectation, the Brahman set out to search for the Buddha. Tracking the footprints, he found the Buddha quietly meditating under a tree. The Buddha had a dignified appearance with a bright light emanating from his body. The Brahman asked nervously, "Are you a celestial being?"

The Buddha replied equably, "No, I am not a celestial being."

"Are you a naga?"

"I am not a naga."

"Are you a yaksa?"

"No, I am not a yaksa."

"Are you a gandharva?"

"No, I am not a gandharva."

"Are you an asura? A garuda? A kinnara? A mahoraga?"

"I am not any of these."

The Brahman then asked with disbelief, "Then you are a man, aren't you?"

The Buddha replied, "I am not a man."

Then the Brahman asked with increasing disbelief, "So... are you saying you are non-human?"

The Buddha said with a smile, "I am not a non-human."

The Brahman asked, wide-eyed, "Then what are you?"

The Buddha answered without haste, "All the creatures you just mentioned are sentient beings that live with afflictions. I have overcome all delusion, broken through the wheel of samsara, and gone beyond the three realms. Therefore, I do not belong to any category of sentient beings that live within the three realms. Although I inherited flesh and blood from my parents, I am not a worldly man inflicted with passions. I am like the blossoms of a lotus plant, white and pure, born from muddy water and yet unsoiled by it. I have cultivated for many kalpas, and in this life I have attained ultimate awakening. Therefore, I am a Buddha."

The Buddha is a perfect person. He has become perfectly awakened and awakened infinite sentient beings. People are simply unawakened Buddhas. Though they are not yet awakened, if they undergo diligent practice, it is possible for them to become Buddhas.

Actions Speak Louder Than Words

One day, a disciple said to the Buddha, "Lord Buddha, you are the greatest teacher in history."

When the Buddha heard him say this, he did not show any pleasure. Instead he asked him, "Have you met all the great teachers in the world?"

"Of course not," said the disciple.

"And do you know all the teachers who are living in the world now, or those who will be born in the future?"

"I do not know them," the disciple answered.

"Well then, when you said that I am the greatest among all teachers, that utterance was meaningless, since you cannot verify the statement."

"I just wanted to praise you, since your teaching is so excellent," the disciple explained.

"If you consider my teachings beneficial, then uphold and practice them. Diligent practice, rather than empty praise, will make me happy."

The Buddha then asked another disciple close by, "If you wanted to buy some gold, would you part with your money before inspecting the gold?"

"Of course not! If the gold is fake, it would be a waste," the disciple answered.

The Buddha continued, "Do not think that something is true and correct because I say it is. You should apply my teachings for yourself to see if they are true. If your experience validates them, then continue your practice. Do not follow my teachings just out of respect for me. Furthermore, do not criticize other people's teachings, or put down others' beliefs. There are many great teachers in this world, and each one of them has a set of methods to help people. You must have no arrogance when dealing with them. Whether they are good teachers or not is not your concern. Your only concern is to free yourself from suffering and to attain happiness, and to help others do the same."

Having listened to the Buddha's teachings, the monks treated everyone with respect.

Adorning Oneself with the Dharma

One day, King Prasenajit and his attendants came to a park where they had often come to pay homage to the Buddha only to find that the Buddha was currently teaching at that very park. The park was secluded and tranquil, and the atmosphere made King Prasenajit feel a strong need to go to where the Buddha was residing and pay homage to him. Thus he ordered his attendants to arrange for a horse and carriage and he went to meet the Buddha at once.

Once King Prasenajit arrived, he sincerely bowed before the Buddha and was very humble. The Buddha asked him, "Your Majesty, why do you display so much formality today? Do you need my service?"

King Prasenajit replied, "For many years I have benefited from listening to your teachings. Recently I have come to understand how much your teachings can stabilize the world and bring harmony to people. I see this in my daily administration of the nation's affairs. When I was in the capital, I saw parents fighting with their children, siblings fighting amongst each other, fathers criticizing their sons, and sons accusing their fathers of stubborness. Their arguments are endless.

"When monks have a difference of opinion or a disagreement within the monastic community, I have never heard them criticize the Buddha, the Dharma, or the Sangha. Instead they criticize themselves for causing problems and attribute it to a lack of virtue or insufficient practice.

"Once I met a Brahman who look very tired. His skin was broken with sores, and his face was pallid and bloodless.

Everyone avoided him, but I approached him and asked, 'Has your conduct been impure? Have you commited unwholesome actions that result in your current appearance?' He was speechless.

"Alternatively, the monks in the sangha all look radiant and spirited. Their dignified appearance commands respect, and they are always neat and clean. They are generous and have no worldly motives. I thought, 'It must be because the monks have the joy of the Dharma in their hearts that their conduct is pure and virtuous.' Therefore, I cannot help but offer praise to the Buddha and his monks.

"In my country there are many Brahmans who constantly boast about their extensive knowledge, their unmatched wit and wisdom, and their great debating skills. They come to your monastery to challenge you in debate and intend to embarrass you but, once they appear before you, they are speechless and eventually take refuge in the Triple Gem. They even vow to observe the five precepts and join the sangha. Your Dharma is a virtuous teaching and the monks are sages that put these teachings into practice.

"I often praised and rewarded two of my ministers, but they pay more reverence to you than to me. Once, I led my troops on an expedition. As I was making the midnight rounds of the military camps, I overheard them discussing your virtuous teachings deep into the night. Eventually, before they went to sleep, one mentioned that you were teaching nearby, and they all turned to face that direction and bowed to you. When they did that, their feet were facing my direction. I was amazed and moved.

"Lord Buddha, I am the king of my land but you are the king of the Dharma. I belong to the warrior caste and so do you. I am eighty year old and so are you. I am willing to pay homage to you, serve you, and to protect the Dharma with all my strength and all my years."

The Buddha is a great sage. His greatness is not measured in his worldy gains, but instead is a natural result of his compassion. He does not seek to gain followers with authority or might. Authority can only make someone follow you super-ficially, but it cannot change someone's mind. The Buddha has set for all of us an example that is as pure and virtuous as the full moon and the night breeze. His outstanding moral accomplishments and great integrity move all sentient beings to pay homage to him and to willingly follow his leadership.

The Five Delightful Paths

Once the Buddha was residing at Jetavana Monastery for the rains retreat. At the end of the retreat, a number of monks gathered together to mend the Buddha's robe. Once his robe was mended the Buddha would leave with his alms-bowl to travel and spread his teachings. When Nandi, of the Sanka Clan, heard that the Buddha would soon be leaving, he went to Jetavana to see the Buddha.

Nandi spoke to the Buddha, "I am growing old – my health is failing and my memory is fading. I am beginning to forget the words you spoke to us. When I heard that the monks were stitching your robe in preparation for your travels, I felt sad because I knew it may be a long time before I would get to see you and your monks again."

The Buddha tried to comfort the old man, and said, "Nandi,

no matter whether or not you see me again, you will always be able to follow the Five Delightful Paths: mindfulness of the Buddha, mindfulness of the Dharma, mindfulness of the Sangha, mindfulness of the precepts, and mindfulness of one's own generosity. Always remember to follow this path in your day to day life."

After hearing the Buddha's words, Nandi was no longer worried. He bowed to the Buddha and left.

Not Yours

One day, the Buddha was teaching in the city of Devadaha. The lord of the city, King Suprabuddha, was the father of Yasodhara. The king was very angry with the Buddha because he had left his beloved daughter and family to seek the path to awakening.

When the Buddha was receiving offerings, the king rudely interfered by blocking all the roads. He yelled at the Buddha, "You should be ashamed to receive offerings in my city! I forbid all citizens from giving you offerings. You abandoned your country, your father and your wife to seek awakening. Though my city has plenty of food, none of it shall go to a person who deserts his country, father, and wife! I command you to leave here immediately!"

The Buddha gently replied, "Please do not blame me. From what you have said, I think there is a misunderstanding. When I left home, I did not abandon my country, my father nor my wife. Instead, I see the entire world as my country and all people as my family. I see every sentient being as my parent, brother, sister, wife and child. I have attained awakening, and with ultimate wisdom I have become a Buddha. I have become one with the universe, and have great compassion for each and every sentient being.

"As the lord of this city, you should love and protect your citizens. As the Buddha, I should love and protect all sentient beings. I have much sympathy for your narrow love; yet selfish love should be discarded when one becomes a Buddha. If you examine it carefully, you will realize that this city is not yours and neither is the food. All that belongs to you is the good and bad karma from your own behavior. Eventually, the people and the food will leave you, but your good and bad karma will follow you until it bears fruit."

Unfortunately, the king was not awakened by the Buddha's words. Although his rudeness was completely tolerated by the Buddha with compassion and magnanimity, one can never escape from the karmic consequence of one's actions according to the law of cause and effect. The king died miserably of a sudden illness within seven days.

When The Mind Is Pure, The Land Is Pure

According to the *Vimalakirti Sutra*, the Venerable Sariputra once suspected that the Buddha's land was not pure.

Sariputra asked the Buddha, "Lord Buddha, why are all the other Buddha's lands pure, and it is only yours that is defiled?"

"You do not know the world in which I live," The Buddha replied. The Buddha then touched his toe to the earth, and Sariputra saw the whole world as pure and majestic: the land became golden and adorned with all sorts of jewels.

The Buddha told Sariputra, "This is the world as I see it."

Sariputra did not understand, and asked, "Why is your vision of the world so different from mine?"

The Buddha gave an example, "Those born blind have never seen the sun and the moon. Yet they should not say that the sun and the moon do not exist. They should place the blame on their blindness."

At this time a celestial being told Sariputra, "Venerable sir, your mind is discriminating. It is not in agreement with the Buddha's wisdom. Therefore you see this world as defiled. Sariputra, bodhisattvas treat all sentient beings equally. Their clear and pure minds are in accordance with the Buddha's wisdom. Thus the bodhisattvas see all lands as pure."

Sariputra still did not understand so the Buddha gave another example, "In heaven, celestial beings' food appears in different colors according to the merit of each individual. Therefore, Sariputra, if one's mind is clear and pure, one can perceive the purity and majesty of this world."

There are people who physically live in luxury yet still feel restless in their minds. There are also people who are happy and content even though they are poor. If one can maintain a pure and clear mind, then the surrounding environment one perceives is always beautiful and pure.

The Light of the Buddha

Once when the Buddha was residing in Sravasti, there was an elder who had been deluded by the wanderers of other sects and did not believe in the Law of Cause and Effect. The Buddha knew this man had a root of goodness and was eager to liberate him from his delusions. So, one day when the elder was walking by Jetavana Monastery, the Buddha appeared before the man sitting under a tree, with rays of light emitting from his body that were illuminating all of Jetavana.

Suddenly the trees turned golden. The elder saw the light and asked someone passing by, "What is this light? I have never seen it before. Do you know what it is?" But the person did not know.

The elder thought for a while and said, "Is this sunlight?"

"No. Sunlight is hot, but this is warm and pleasant. It is not sunlight," the person answered.

"Then is this light from a fire?"

"No, light from a fire would flicker, but this light is steady. It is surely not a fire," the person answered. The elder was speechless.

After a while he asked again, "Then what is this light?"

The person said, "Oh! This must be the wander Gautama's virtuous radiance."

"Nonsense. I do not like this kind of talk." Enraged, the elder started to head home in his cart.

At this time the Buddha used his supernatural power to close all the exits to the outside road except the one leading by Jetavana Monastery. The elder was frightened and thought he had no way out. Reluctantly he turned back and headed directly toward the Buddha. Unable to avoid the Buddha, he covered his face with a fan. However, the power of the Buddha exposed the elder completely, leaving him no place to hide. When he lifted his head, he came face to face with the Buddha. When the elder saw the dignified and kind Buddha and thought of his great power, he came out of his cart and bowed. The Buddha then taught the elder the Dharma. The elder felt as if he had found a light in the darkness. From that point forward, he followed the right path.

With great kindness and compassion, the Buddha blesses even those who do not wish to be close to him. He will liberate anyone who is ready to follow the Way.

The Five Difficulties in Human Life

After the Buddha became awakened, he set out for Varanasi, to teach the Dharma to his five former ascetic disciples. While he was traveling he met a Brahman on the road. He had left his parents and his hometown and was seeking good teachers to learn the Way. When he met the Buddha, he saw the Buddha's magnificent appearance and felt a strong admiration in his heart. He praised the Buddha and asked, "How did you learn the Way? Who is your teacher? How did you gain the dignified appearance of a sage?"

The Buddha told him, "I have become awakened and have removed myself from the net of desire. I have developed a mind that is free of delusion. I have no teacher."

Then the Brahman asked the Buddha, "Where are you going?"

The Buddha said, "I am going to the country of Sravasti to

beat the drum of the Dharma and turn the wheel of Truth. I am going to teach the multitudes the way of liberation from birth and death."

After hearing what the Buddha said, the Brahman was very pleased and said to the Buddha, "This is wonderful! I would also like to hear about the Dharma and to know how I can free myself from birth and death. However, I have something else I need to do first, and I must now go and take care of these concerns. In the future, I would like to listen to the Dharma." The Brahman then left the Buddha. Unfortunately, before he could listen to the Dharma again he became gravely ill and died.

The Buddha, with his celestial vision, saw that the Brahman he had met on the road had died. With sympathy, he said, "People in this world are ignorant. They do not understand impermanence and they think there will be plenty of time to do what they intend. They think they can wait to learn the Dharma. Take the Brahman I met shortly after my awakening: he met with the Buddha, yet he still missed the opportunity to learn the Dharma. Now he is dead and can no longer listen to the Dharma. He will continue to wander through the six realms without knowing how to gain liberation from suffering."

The Buddha then taught his disciples the five difficulties in human life, which are:

1. It is difficult to gain a human birth.
2. Once born as a human, it is difficult to live a long life.
3. Once alive, it is difficult to be born at a time when a Buddha is living in the human world.
4. It is difficult to be able to listen to the Dharma.
5. If one hears the Dharma, it is difficult to have faith in the Dharma.

The Afflictions of The Golden Body

When we look at the Buddha, he is dignified and elegant. We can be easily misled into thinking that the Buddha never experienced any obstacles or misfortunes while living in this world.

Through his physical appearance, the Buddha was revealing to us the truth about worldly existence. There is a saying, "Teaching through example is more important than teaching through words." Since the Buddha taught the truth about suffering, impermanence, and non-self, it would be contradictory if he remained young and healthy. This was why he wanted to demonstrate that in this world, even a Buddha endowed with a graceful human form, must undergo suffering and misfortune.

The Buddha had two accidents while on the road. The first one happened when he was walking and his foot was pierced by a large piece of wood from a poisonous tree. The second time was when his toe was injured by a giant rock deliberately pushed down by Devadatta.

The Buddha also fell ill twice. Once he fell ill with dysentery, and asked the physician Jivaka to prescribe medicine for him. The Buddha also suffered from back pain. The Buddha asked Ananda to collect some milk for him as alms, and asked Mahakasyapa to chant for him the *Seven Limbs of Enlightenment*. Thus his back pain was finally relieved.

There were two other times when the Buddha had difficulty in collecting alms. The first time was during a period of famine. Over a period of three months, the Buddha subsisted only on horse food. The second time occurred when the Buddha had to go hungry for a day and night, having failed to obtain any food from his alms round.

Once a Brahman woman sneered at the Buddha to his face. King Suprabuddha also criticized the Buddha, with his contemptuous finger pointing straight at his sagely figure. Although the Buddha did not mind these afflictions, all these people suffered the negative karmic effects of their actions. A great religious leader must have the character to challenge any disaster.

As the Buddha met with such misfortunes, all those who had not grasped the true meaning of the Dharma could easily become skeptical. One day, king Prasenajit asked the Buddha, "Lord Buddha, we have no doubt regarding your handsome appearance and dignified conduct, but why is it that, during your life of teaching, you have had several misfortunes?"

The Buddha replied, "Your Majesty, all the Buddhas have an everlasting Dharma body. Yet, I have manifested in this body for the purpose of liberating all sentient beings. My bodily injuries, my need for medicine to cure my illnesses, my parinirvana, my future relics for people to pay homage to, all these are skillful means for you to realize the existence of karma. Hopefully, everyone who lives in fear of bad karma, will cease to do what is unwholesome and practice what is wholesome so that they can acquire a Dharma body. Everyone should aspire to the Dharma body, which is pure and boundless, rather than cling to this world of conditioned physical existence."

Upon hearing this, King Prasenajit's suspicions dissipated. He was overwhelmed with joy. Not only did he now recognize the dignified appearance of the Buddha, but his great compassion as well.

The Turning of the Dharma Wheel

Soon after the Buddha became awakened there were many who discriminated against his teachings. The discrimination of the wanderers from other sects was the most extreme. However, the number of people who learned the Dharma and began to apply it in their daily lives slowly grew. Their lives became significant, hopeful, prosperous, harmonious, and happy.

The Buddha's teachings gradually earned a good reputation that spread far and wide and attracted many people who had admiration for the Dharma and a thirst to learn. Certain disciples who had also attained awakening and were equally capable of teaching the Dharma started to come to the fore. The Buddha then began to send out these disciples in every direction to teach the Dharma.

He told these disciples, "For the Dharma and Discipline to grow we need to propagate them. They should never be left in silence. This teaching is superb and full of truth and should not fall into the hands of those who do not value it or insult it, discriminate against it, belittle it, or criticize it. Go now and teach the Dharma to those who are eager to learn, and transmit the precepts to those you approve of. Now go! In order to save the world with compassion and for the benefit of all sentient beings, disseminate the wondrous Dharma that is perfect in both its meaning and phrasing. People's eyes are obscured by the dust of earthly phenomena. They will never be liberated if they do not receive the Dharma. As long as you teach them peacefully and with patience they will naturally abide by the Way and not stray from it."

From that point forward, there was a new rule within the sangha: on clear days the monks were to go out and teach the Dharma, while on rainy days they were to gather in the monastery and listen to the Buddha's teaching.

It is people that propagate the Dharma rather than the Dharma that propagates people. It takes the hands of Buddhist disciples to make the wheel of Dharma turn in the human world. It is only through the efforts of Buddhist followers that Buddhism can continue to be known in this human world. The responsibility to glorify the Buddha's teachings are shouldered by every Humanistic Buddhist bodhisattva.

Seeing the Dharma Is Seeing the Buddha

It says in the *Salistamba Sutra*, "If one sees the Dependent Origination, one sees the Dharma; when one sees the Dharma, one sees the Buddha." This does not apply only to those who were fortunate enough to live at the time of the Buddha, but also to every Buddhist follower.

Once, a follower of the Buddha named Vakula suddenly fell ill. He knew he did not have long to live and entrusted those who looked after him to inform the Buddha of his situation. Since he was unable to return to the monastery, he wished that the Buddha would come to him so that he could pay homage to the Buddha before he died.

To honor Vakula's wish, the Buddha immediately made his way to his home. Upon the Buddha's arrival, Vakula tried to struggle out of bed to pay homage to him. When he saw this, the Buddha persuaded Vakula to lie down instead. He sat at his bedside, and kindly inquired about his illness.

Vakula said, "Lord Buddha, my condition worsens day by day. I am afraid I will not recover. I just wanted to see you one more time before I died."

The Buddha replied, "Vakula, seeing some old, frail body is useless. You should realize that seeing the Dharma is seeing me, and that seeing me is seeing the Dharma. That is why you should recollect the Dharma that I have taught instead of me."

On hearing this, Vakula suddenly attain awakening. He was moved to tears and considered it a blessing bestowed on him to be able to hear the Buddha's teachings even in the final moments of his life. All the other followers who were present were deeply touched and could not help but praise the Buddha for being so compassionate.

Carrying His Father's Coffin

After the Buddha attained awakening, news of this quickly reached Kapilavatsu, and the happiest person to learn of this was none other than that Buddha's father, King Suddhodana. Once the Buddha arrived at Jetavana Monastery, having taught all the way from the south, King Suddhodana quickly sent his minister Udayin to welcome the early return of the Buddha to his home country.

Soon afterwards, the Buddha returned with a large number of his disciples to teach the Dharma to his father and his ministers. It was at this time that the Buddha's cousins, such as Devadatta, Ananda, Aniruddha, and Bhadrika, were inspired to leave home and follow the Buddha.

After staying for three months, the Buddha returned to Jetavana Monastery with his followers. Several years passed before he returned to Vulture Peak in Rajagrha for the rains retreat. One day, King Suddhodana sent his messenger to inform the Buddha that he had fallen seriously ill and that he wished to see the Buddha one last time.

Without delay, the Buddha immediately left for Kapilavatsu with Nanda, Ananda, and Rahula after giving simple instruct-ions to the rest of his disciples.

Although the king was already ninety-three years old and very ill, he was still aware of the Buddha's return. With a sad smile, he slowly extended his hand. Silently, the Buddha stepped forward to hold his father's hand.

Nanda was sobbing, and Ananda and Rahula could not stop their tears. All the palace maids cried bitterly. In a very feeble voice, the king said, "Please do not feel sorrow. The Buddha has said that all things are impermanent. I feel truly happy now that my son has become the ultimately noble Buddha. He has accomplished his original vow from many kalpas ago, and apart from taking this as the glory of my life, I have been blessed with great comfort and contentment. This is the final moment of my life, and to see the Buddha one last time is like catching a glimpse of life after death."

With his palms joined and a smile on his face, King Suddhodana passed away.

Still remaining silent, the Buddha solemnly watched his father pass away. Although all beings have their own karma, King Suddhodana attained a certain degree of nirvana due to the Buddha's great virtue.

The body of King Suddhodana was cleaned, oiled and embalmed before being placed in a coffin, which was ornamented with jewels and placed in the center of the palace. Curtains adorned with pearls were draped around it and flowers were scattered all around. The Buddha and Nanda sat near the front of the coffin, while Ananda and Rahula sat near the back.

During the night, Nanda pleaded with the Buddha, "Lord Buddha, at the funeral tomorrow, I implore you to let me carry the coffin."

On hearing this, Ananda and Rahula made similar requests, and the Buddha replied, "Very well, I will carry the coffin as well."

The funeral of King Suddhodana was solemn and dignified, and many treasures were donated to the poor and needy. Everyone in the country mourned the king's death. On the day of the funeral, everyone present was moved to tears as they saw the Buddha carrying his father's coffin towards the funeral pyre. Each one of them paid homage to the Buddha by kneeling at the roadside.

By carrying the coffin of his father, the Buddha had not only fulfilled his filial duty, but also established an exemplary filial act for his future followers.

The Tears of the Buddha

One day, a demon said to the Buddha, "We dislike how well known your teachings have become. From now on, we will fight against you."

The Buddha replied without the slightest concern, "No matter how destructive you are, I will not be afraid."

"Wherever we go, we will criticize and slander you."

The Buddha said calmly, "This does not frighten me."

"We will bear arms and attack you."

"I am not afraid of any weapon."

Seeing that the Buddha was not threatened, the demon said, "Then we will become your disciples. We will wear monastic robes and eat your food, but we will not observe your teachings. When you speak of discipline, meditative concentration, and wisdom, we will act with greed, anger, and ignorance. We will do everything to oppose your teachings. This is the way to destroy you."

When the Buddha heard this, he was filled with pity for all the suffering of sentient beings in the age of the declining Dharma. Hurtful tears were shed. At last, the Buddha cried.

It is frightening for any community to experience external threats, but oppression from the outside can germinate solidarity against an enemy. What is most frightening is when there is internal discord. When those within a community sabotage or antagonize each other, the whole community or organization will be dismantled in the long run. This is what makes internal dissent so frightening.

In today's society, many people claim to be Buddhist followers, wave the Buddhist banner, and wear monastic robes, but do not act in accordance with Buddhist principles, thereby putting Buddhism in disrepute. Consider the saying, "The insects who seek shelter on the lion's body turn to feed on the lion." A family can lose its fortune if they raise an unfilial child. A country, no matter how great its power, finds it hard to deal with traitors. When children do not listen to their parents' advice, the parents will be deeply hurt. When faced with followers who violated Buddhist principles, the Buddha finally could not control his tears.

Part Five:

Supernatural Powers

The mind holds untold power, and when it is focused the mind is capable of miraculous feats. The Buddhist sutras are full of stories of these kinds of supernatural powers, where people bend the world to their will.

The Buddha, whose own supernatural powers were equal to none, did not use them to dazzle or amaze, but to teach the Dharma to sentient beings. These stories show the failure of supernatural powers when they are used for the wrong reasons, and the impact upon those who felt the Buddha's incredible power.

Crossing the Ganges

Once, the Buddha was walking to the Ganges River when it suddenly began to flood, making it impossible to tread across the river. While the Buddha was observing the situation, a boatman rowed by and asked, "Do you want to cross the river?"

"Yes. Would you take me across the river?"

"Yes, but you must pay me first."

The Buddha then told the boatman compassionately, "Boatman, members of our sangha have only three robes and an alms bowl. We live a simple life in the pursuit of awakening. Where would I get money for boat fare? I have freed myself from the bondage of affliction, and see all treasures as ordinary rocks and soil. I do not carry any money with me."

This boatman was very greedy and the Buddha's sincerity failed to move him. He said stubbornly, "Well, since you do not have any money, I cannot ferry you across. I'm sorry."

He then started to row his boat away from the shore. Suddenly, the Buddha saw a flock of geese flying across the sky toward the opposite bank. The Buddha said to the boatman, "Watch the flock of geese as they use their own natural powers to fly anywhere they wish. They need not ask a boatman how much the fare is and no one dares ask them to pay. I shall use my supernatural powers to fly across the river like those geese."

As soon as the Buddha finished speaking he appeared on the other shore. When the boatman witnessed the Buddha's supernatural powers, he felt ashamed. He pounded his chest, stamped his feet, and said, "How unfortunate for me! Though I was able to meet the Buddha and had the opportunity to plant good seeds for the future, I failed to make offerings to him. I don't know if I will ever see the Buddha again. I shall fall into unfortunate rebirths forever!" Shortly afterward, he fainted and remained unconscious for a long time. Everyone who saw or heard of this incident felt sorry for the boatman.

Later on, the boatman reported the incident to King Bimbisara of the Magadha Kingdom. The king issued a decree, "From now on, all sangha members can ride boats without having to pay fares. All boatmen must respectfully ferry the sangha members." With this decree, the Buddha and his disciples were able to travel conveniently everywhere to teach the Dharma.

Denouncing Supernatural Power

Pindola-bharadvaja, the arhat with bushy eyebrows, was one of the sixteen principal followers of the Buddha mentioned in *The Amitabha Sutra*. He was an arhat who had attained spiritual accomplishment. At one time, he revealed his supernatural powers to a group of Buddhist followers and received their applause. Encouraged, Pindola said to his spect-ators, "Is flying through the sky amazing enough for you? I will show it to you now! It will truly be an experience for all who are gathered here!" He then jumped from the ground, flew to the middle of the sky, and there performed other supernatural acts. The crowd was awed by his power and cheered in wonderment.

Having been informed of this, the Buddha was greatly displeased with the monk's behavior. He sent for Pindola and admonished him, "My teachings aim to inspire others by our discipline, virtue, and our commitment to liberating all sentient beings. This does not include using supernatural powers to excite crowds and delude the public. You used your supernatural powers to win people's devotion— this is an abuse which cannot stand. You will remain in this mundane world of suffering and hardship until you accumulate enough merit to eliminate your bad karma. Only then will you reach nirvana."

Even though Pindola had become an arhat he remained in this world. He could not enter nirvana. This story advises us that Buddhism does not emphasize supernatural power. Buddhism is a religion that is based on discipline, compassion, and wisdom.

Taming a Mad Elephant

Devadatta was a monk who wished to displace the Buddha as the leader of the sangha. Thus Devadatta was constantly coming up with schemes to murder the Buddha.

One day, the Buddha led his disciples with their alms-bowls outside the city of Rajagrha to collect alms. Suddenly a mad drunken elephant charged towards the Buddha and his disciples. When the monks saw it coming they were frightened and quickly ran for cover. They implored the Buddha to run away and avoid the violent onslaught of the mad elephant.

But the Buddha said calmly, "Monks, do not be frightened. One who has attained Buddhahood will not allow himself to be harmed or killed by external violence."

As the Buddha spoke, the mad elephant drew nearer him. Once the elephant was close enough to see the Buddha it knelt down and became tame. The Buddha taught the elephant about taking refuge in the Triple Gem. As the elephant listened, tears flowed down from its eyes. Thus, Devadatta's plan to murder the Buddha with a mad elephant, did not succeed.

A Spider's Thread

Although people regard the Buddha as an almighty being with supernatural powers, he also had his moments when he was unable to help people.

Once there was a villain named Kandata. Everything he did in his life was evil. The only good thing he did in his entire life was when we saw a spider as he was walking down the road. He was about to step on the spider but, in a moment of kindness he realized that the spider would die if he stepped on it. He quickly withdrew his foot and the poor creature was saved.

Kandata's evil conduct led him to be reborn in hell after his death. The spider that he had spared when he was alive wanted to repay his kindness. In order to fulfill the wish of the little creature, the Buddha helped the spider drop his thread into hell to try to save Kandata. All the suffering beings in hell were very happy to see the thread. They all wanted to leave hell desperately, so they each made a dash for the thread.

Upon seeing this, anger arose in Kandata's heart and he mercilessly pushed others away, shouting, "Go away! This is my spider thread! Only I can use it to get out of here! Go away!"

He violently grabbed for the thread, but the tiny thread could not bear the strain and broke. All the suffering beings fell back into hell again, including Kandata. The Buddha heaved a helpless sigh, "What a pity! With their selfishness and anger, these sentient beings refuse to share even the slightest benefit or to be compassionate with one another. Even with my determination to save them, my efforts were in vain."

Hiding From Death

In Rajagrha there lived four Brahman brothers who had supernatural powers. They could fly through the air, dive below the surface of the earth, move mountains and oceans, and even hold dominion over the sun and the moon. Through their supernatural powers, they knew that they each only had seven days to live but they thought that, since there was nothing on earth that they could not do, they believed they could escape death.

Therefore, the first brother said, "I will dive into the sea and will not rise to the surface nor sink to the bottom. I will just dive and swim inbetween the two. This way death will not be able to find me."

The second brother said, "I will penetrate deep into Mt. Sumeru. This way death will not be able to find me."

The third brother said, "I will hide in deep in the vastness of space. This way death will not be able to find me."

The fourth brother said, "I will mingle in a big crowd in a busy city. This way, death will catch someone else by mistake."

Upon finishing their discussion, the four brothers went to the king of Magadha to bid him farewell, "Your Majesty, we only have seven days left on earth. We are each going to try to escape death and find a safe place to hide for the next seven days. After seven days have elapsed, we will come back to greet you again. While we are gone, we hope that you acquire merit by loving your people and protecting the country."

After they departed each brother followed his plan to avoid

death. Despite their plans, after seven days passed, all four brothers died, just as ripened fruit drops to the ground when its time has come.

When the king learned that one of the brothers was found dead in the street, he knew that the other three would fail to escape death as well. The king approached the Buddha for advice, "In my country, there were four brothers whose supernatural powers were so incredible that they knew their lives were about to end. They even tried to escape impending death. Please tell me if such an escape is ever possible."

The Buddha replied, "In life, there are four things that cannot be avoided: one will be born, one will grow old, one will be tortured by sickness, and eventually one will die. One cannot possibly escape death."

After listening to the Buddha's advice, the king praised the Buddha, "Excellent, I understand your teachings. The four Brahman brothers' attempt to use their supernatural powers to escape death could not succeed. All worldly success, fame and longevity are subject to karma. One of the brothers has been confirmed dead, the other three also will not be able to escape the forces of karma."

As an old saying goes, "The one beaten to death is the one who knows how to fight, and the one drowned is the one who knows how to swim." Do not think that supernatural powers are almighty and that there is nothing to fear. When the force of karma ripens, supernatural powers can do nothing. If one solely relies on such powers, one can make things worse and possibly even die.

The Liberation of an Ugly Man

In Sravasti, there was an elder who had a son who was so ugly that everyone was scared of him. He eventually became a recluse in the woods to avoid running into people and scaring them. He survived by foraging in the woods for wild fruits.

The Buddha knew this man's situation and wanted to liberate him from his sufferings, so he took his disciples to the woods where the man was staying. The man fled as the Buddha approached. Thus, the Buddha turned himself into a dirty and ugly person and walked toward the ugly man with a bowl of food in his hand.

While the elder pondered the situation, the Buddha walked towards him in his new ugly form. Though the ugly man was initially disturbed, he was then glad to see another person like himself in the woods. He could not help but walk up to the Buddha and tell him, "We are both unkempt, ugly, and lonely. We could become good friends, couldn't we?"

"Yes, we could. We should cooperate like brothers. I would like to offer you my bowl of food."

The ugly man knew then that he had found a genuine friend. He was very happy and shared in the Buddha's food without hesitation. After the meal, the ugly man was very surprised when his friend suddenly became neat and handsome. He asked curiously, "How have you suddenly become a totally different person, and are now majestic and elegant?"

The Buddha said slowly, "It is very simple. During the meal, I observed the monks meditating under the tree over there with compassion and respect. Thus I naturally became neat and handsome."

"Is it really that easy? Life is so difficult for an ugly man. I wish I could be a normal looking person."

"Why do you not try?"

The ugly man felt he had discovered a great treasure and his heart was filled with gladness. Completely trusting in what the Buddha said, he observed the meditating monks with a compassionate gaze and a kind mind.

The Buddha then returned to his original appearance, bearing the thirty two marks of excellence and the eighty noble qualities. The brightness of the Buddha radiated like the light of a thousand suns. Without thinking, the ugly man bowed before the Buddha and said, "I ridiculed and scolded Buddhists in my previous lives. Now I am experiencing the effects of that bad karma. To repent my previous deeds, I would like to become a monk and study the Dharma."

"Excellent!" the Buddha said gladly, "I shall accept you as one of my disciples."

Instantly, the man's beard and hair fell off and he simultaneously appeared as a monk draped in monastic robes. The Buddha then taught the Dharma to him.

The ugly man dedicated himself to following the Buddha's teachings and studied the Dharma diligently. He soon became an arhat and no longer suffered from his ugliness.

Auspicious Grass

An old woman was stricken with grief because she had just lost her son. Overtaken by sadness, she suddenly remembered that the Buddha was fully awakened and that he might be able to bring her son back to life. Therefore, she went to pay homage to the Buddha full of hope.

When the old woman saw the compassionate Buddha, like a drowning person who has suddenly found a life raft, she was on her knees saying, "Lord Buddha, I have learned that you are mighty, compassionate, and like a father for all sentient beings. You are able to help sentient beings solve all kinds of problems. I once had a very lovely boy, but he passed away and left me all alone in this world. Please bring him back to life for his pitiful mother. If you bring him back, I will become your follower and support and protect the Dharma. Otherwise, I will not put my faith in your teachings."

The Buddha felt no anger for the old woman's unreasonable request. He responded compassionately, "There is a kind of medicinal herb somewhere in the world called 'auspicous grass.' If you can find it, you can bring your son back to life."

When the old woman heard of such a wonderful herb, she asked urgently, "May I please ask, where can I find this auspicious grass?"

"Auspicious grass only grows in a household where no one has ever died. Hurry and go search for it!" the Buddha answered.

The old woman tried in vain to find a household where no one had ever died. She went from door-to-door and looked from dawn to dusk. She could never find what she was looking for, though she traveled through many countries. After searching for a long period of time, she found that it was impossible to find a single dwelling where no one had ever died. She found herself in an abyss of hopelessness and desperation. Suddenly, she realized that death is a path that every living being has to go along on one's journey. Because of the Buddha's skillful teaching, the old woman finally extricated herself from the deep grief of losing her son, and started anew.

In this world all things come into being and fade away; they come together and break apart. Human beings journey through a process of birth, old age, sickness and death. Life and death are only briefest of moments on a cosmic scale. The continuous cycle of birth and death and construction and destruction are a part of nature. Once we understand the rationale behind these continuous cycles, we will learn to experience and comprehend the meaning of infinite life.

Ullambana

The Venerable Maudgalyayana had the supernatural power to see the karmic causes which led to the suffering of ghosts and spirits.

One day, he suddenly thought of his deceased mother. Using his supernatural powers, he saw his mother undergoing immense torture in the realm of the hungry ghosts. Her throat was as tiny as a pinhole, and her bones and skin had melded into one. On witnessing the state of his mother, Maudgalyayana was extremely saddened. He filled his bowl with rice and vegetables and hoped to be able to feed his mother through his supernatural powers. The rice had hardly reached his mother's lips when it was transformed into red hot coal, making it impossible to swallow.

Maudgalyayana started to cry uncontrollably. Even though he had the ability to know why ghosts had come to the realm of hungry ghosts, he could not see the karmic cause for his mother. Heavy-hearted, Maudgalyayana came to the Buddha for advice, "Lord Buddha, I have witnessed my mother from my present life suffering in the realm of hungry ghosts. Whatever food she tried to eat was transformed into fire. What is the karmic cause of this? I can see others' karma with my supernatural power. Why can I not see that of my own mother? Please teach me."

The Buddha's face emanated the radiance of compassion when he replied, "Maudgalyayana! Your mother used to slander the Buddha and the sangha when she was alive. She did not believe in the Law of Cause and Effect nor in the Dharma. She was greedy, angry and had false views. These are the reasons for her present suffering. As you are blinded by your deep affection for your mother, you cannot see the karmic cause of this."

"Lord Buddha, is there any wasy that I can help my mother escape from the torment of being a hungry ghost?" Maudgalyayana pleaded with the Buddha.

"Maudgalyayana, your mother's wrongdoing is too great to be saved by your power alone. Although your filial piety has moved heaven and earth, the celestial beings cannot excuse those who slander the Triple Gem. All you can do now is rely on the power of the sangha to liberate your mother from her suffering.

"On the fifteenth day of the seventh lunar month of every year, the last day of the rains retreat, men and women of righteous families should make offerings of exquisite food and fresh fruits to the sangha for the sake of their parents in this and their past seven lives.

"On this day all sagely beings will either meditate by the hills and rivers and obtain samadhi, become arhats, recite the sutras, or attain supernatural powers and freely spread the Dharma. The bodhisattvas of the ten directions may appear as monks and receive your offerings. These sages uphold the precepts with such purity that their merit is unimaginable. If one takes the opportunity to make offerings to them, one's parents and relatives will be freed from the suffering of the three lower realms and be able to obtain food and clothing without difficulty. For those parents who are still alive, they will enjoy good fortune and comfort for many years to come. This is the way to liberate them."

Maudgalyayana was delighted with the Buddha's teaching. He did as he was instructed on that day of the year, and his mother was liberated from the pain and suffering of the hungry ghosts.

Maudgalyayana felt great gratitude toward the Buddha and praised the merit of the Triple Gem. He persuaded everyone to do the same on the fifteenth day of the seventh lunar month every year to repay their parents for the benevolence of their love and upbringing.

Maudgalyayana's original intention of asking everyone to do as he did on Ullambana was for the benefit of all beings. Unfortunately, people have mistaken the fifteenth day of the seventh lunar month as just a day for worshipping ghosts and spirits, thereby misapplying the loving-kindness and compassion of the Buddha and Maudgalyayana. Nevertheless, Maudgalyayana was known from then on not only for his supernatural powers, but also for his great filial piety.

PART SIX:

LIVING IN COMMUNITY

The Buddha entered this world, attained awakening in this world, and taught the Dharma in this world for the benefit of all sentient beings. His teachings are not only about improving oneself, but about living in this world, improving our relationships, and cultivating how we treat one another.

One cannot practice the Buddha's teachings in isolation, but must live in community with all sentient beings. These stories show us the joys and the responsibilities of being a part of this community.

Aniruddha in the Forest

Once, a great dispute broke out among the Buddha's disciples. The Buddha then told them a story about bearing insult and distress without resentment and urged them to stop fighting. He told them, "Using anger to confront anger will never end this. Only kindness, compassion, patience and endurance can put out the fires of anger."

The Buddha's words touched many of the monks and their anger subsided. Still, there were a few who would not quit arguing with each other. This made the Buddha long for Aniruddha's company. Aniruddha was a monk with great patience. At that time, he was practicing in a forest, so the Buddha went to see him.

In addition to Aniruddha, there were two other monastics practicing in the same forest with him named Bhadra and Kalpina. Together the three lived like brothers. They knew each other well before they left the home life and together the three agreed to follow the Buddha's teachings to awakening.

Aniruddha had already become an arhat and had the supernatural power of the celestial eye. Bhadra and Kalpina also eventually attained awakening, and the three sages lived together happily.

They had agreed to maintain silence except during the meetings which they held every five days to discuss how to learn and improve their practice. Each day, they went out to collect alms. Whoever returned first would lay out the sitting mat, pump the water, and ready the bowl and towel for washing feet. He would then eat his food and save the rest in a cool place or in clean water for those who came back later. When he had finished, he would wash his hands and feet, sit on the sitting mat, and begin to meditate or recite the Buddha's name.

The second person to return ate the food he brought back plus the surplus of the first person's, if needed. He would then save the rest of food for the last person. The last person to return would wash the utensils and clean the eating space. The second and last person to return would also wash their hands and feet and then sit on the sitting mat to meditate after eating.

At the end of the day, the one who finished his meditation first would prepare the water. If he needed help carrying the water tank, he would signal it by hand. Their life was thus peaceful and full of tranquility.

The Buddha went to the forest where the three sages were staying by himself, without his usual company of followers. A man who looked after the three sages did not recognize the Buddha and tried to stop him from going any further so that he would not disturb the three sages. The Buddha assured the man that he would be warmly welcomed by the three.

Indeed, they were pleasantly surprised to see the Buddha, and they rushed out to welcome him. Aniruddha took the Buddha's alms-bowl, Bhadra laid out the sitting mat, and Kalpina prepared water for him to wash his feet.

"Aniruddha, how is your practice? Do you lack anything?" the Buddha asked after he settled down.

"Lord Buddha, our practice is to cut off delusion and follow your teachings, and we are successful in this. Therefore, we feel rich and satisfied. We do not lack anything," Aniruddha answered. Bhadra and Kalpina both expressed the same opinion.

The Buddha said to them, "You three practice together peacefully without fighting. This is the most wonderful way of life." Coming from the disharmonious assembly to this peaceful group, the Buddha was especially delighted. The three monks were gladdened by their teacher's visit too.

One who has the Dharma in mind is the richest person in the world. The Dharma is a treasure of unlimited resources for you to explore in order to calm your mind.

Selfishness Leads to Suffering

Once there was a nun who would always give advice to others. She would warn and caution others away from things to satisfy her own greed and prevent others from sharing her gains.

Even though she had joined the sangha, she disregarded all the monastic rules and would overindulge in eating. She liked to go alone to a certain village that had excellent food to receive offerings so that she could enjoy them all to herself. She was so captured by the delicious flavors that she thought, "If all the other nuns go there to collect alms food, there will be nothing left for me. I must find a way to prevent them from doing so."

Thus she returned to the nun's residence and warned them, "Elder nuns, do not go near this village to collect alms food. There are angry elephants, wild horses and mean dogs all around it. It is too dangerous there."

The other nuns listened to her advice and nobody went to that village to collect alms.

One day, the heedless nun went to her favorite village to collect alms food. As she approached a house, a mad dog attacked her and broke her leg.

The villagers came and took care of her at once. Later when they carried her back to her monastery, the other nuns were confused as to why she went to that village despite her previous warning. Soon, the whole sangha had figured out selfish intentions and discussed her immorality.

When the Buddha heard this, he gathered his disciples and told them, "Even in a previous life, this nun possessed the habit of giving false warnings. She was once a selfish bird when I was the leader of her flock. Once, when I was leading the flock towards a mountain, we stopped and rested in a forest along the way. During the day, all the birds went out looking for food in the forest. She, however, purposely flew to the main road where she found a lot of rice, beans and fruit to enjoy for herself.

"To prevent the other birds from sharing in her discovery, she came back to the forest and warned us, 'The traffic on the main road is horrible, there are elephants, horses, and wagons passing by all the time. We could easily get killed there.'

"Naturally, the warning kept the rest of the flock from going to the main road. She, on the other hand, went back there again. While she was collecting food on the road, she heard a wagon roaring in the distance. She underestimated the speed of the wagon, was unable to fly away in time, and was run over by the wagon.

"One who gives false warning or advice will receives the karmic effects of his selfishness."

After listening to the Buddha's teaching, all his disciples realized the negative impact of selfishness and practiced diligently.

The Difficult Disciple

The sangha is a community which emphasizes harmony. The sangha embraces all types of people. Thus, it is inevitable that some monastics are difficult to discipline and occasionally cause friction within the community.

One particular monk had been a disciple of the Buddha for several years, but he was still an undisciplined young man. He was arrogant and had a bad temperament. He would intentionally oppose other's views and fight with them. He especially liked to speak ill of others and, as a result, many people didn't like him. The Buddha reprimanded him several times. The difficult disciple realized the others didn't like him, so he asked the Buddha to let him go somewhere else to practice.

The Buddha kindly said to him, "I do not object to you practicing elsewhere, but before you leave listen to this story: There was once a crow who decided to leave his fellow crows because no one liked him. While he was flying to live somewhere else, he ran into a magpie. The magpie asked him, 'Crow, where are you flying to?' The crow replied, 'Anywhere. The others don't like me, and I hate living with them as well. I am flying to another place to live.' The magpie said to crow, 'You don't need to move. The others don't like you because you do not have a pleasant song. If you don't change your voice, it doesn't matter where you go, it will always be the same situation.'"

As the Buddha finished the story, he looked at the difficult disciple, "If you don't change your habits, you are just like that crow, not welcome wherever you go. Do you want to be like that crow?"

After listening to the Buddha's story, the disciple realized that he must repent for all his wrongdoing, so he asked the Buddha to give him a chance to correct his shortcomings.

The Buddha saw that he was sincere and told him, "Habits form slowly over time. Some are carried over from past lives, and some are from this life. It is only by the strength of your practice that you can eliminate vexation. Making vows to improve oneself is like removing a weed by the roots. Scraping the top of a weed with a rock is not the ultimate cure. If we weed without removing the roots they will only come back again. Only by removing the roots, can we have an ultimate cure."

By listening to Buddha's compassionate advice, the disciple's mind grew stronger and he became recommitted to his practice. He made a vow to practice diligently to meet the Buddha's expectations.

The Hopeless

Once there was an alcoholic who would lose his reason and do awful, unforgivable deeds when drunk. His friends had left him, and he lost all credibility. He tried to stop drinking when he was sober, but he was never able to resist the temptation of alcohol. He thought that he was hopeless, so he went to the Buddha to ask for help.

The Buddha told him compassionately that, while drinking was a vice, all hope was not lost, "If you make up your mind to stop drinking, you still have a chance. There are only five kinds of people who are truly hopeless."

"What kind of people?" the man asked seriously.

"First are those who flatter others to further themselves.

Second are those who have an evil mind and are cruel. Third are those who speak with sharp forked tongues. Fourth are those who are greedy and jealous. Fifth are those who are not grateful for what they have in life."

The Buddha continued, "If you do not wish to become one of these hopeless people, you should guard your actions, speech, and mind against greed, anger, and delusion. Always be mindful and have no jealousy. Speak compassionately so that every word praises, encourages and cares for people. Never forget any kind deed and always try to return the favor. Never broadcast the faults of others or speak of them in a derogatory manner in order to further yourself. If you are careful and follow these guidelines, you will never become a hopeless person."

After listening to the Buddha's teachings, his disciples all worked hard to become good, compassionate, humble, and generous human beings.

The Buddha Visits the Sick

Once when the Buddha was staying at Jetavana Monastery, a monk became seriously ill. Since he had been bedridden for a long time his living quarters had become filthy. When he first became ill he had many visitors to care for him but, as time went on, fewer and fewer people came to see him.

The Buddha learned of the situation and went to visit the sick monk. Upon entering his living quarters he asked, "You are very sick, is there anyone to take care of you?"

The sick monk weakly replied, "Lord Buddha, many people came to see me at first. As my illness persisted, they stopped coming."

"How are you feeling now?" the Buddha asked.

"Lord Buddha, it has been so hard for me, I don't know if I can ever recover," the monk said with tears in his eyes.

Having heard this, the Buddha touched the monk's body with his hand. Instantly, the monk's illness left him, and he was cured by the incredible power of the Buddha.

"My heartfelt gratitude to you, Lord Buddha! You cured my illness. Please tell me, as a wretched person who was forsaken by all, why do I deserve your compassion?"

"Helping one another is the meaning of community." When the Buddha said this, his face was shining with kindness.

"But, Lord Buddha, I never helped you in the past."

"You have. Since you have not yet attained awakening, you cannot know what has happened in your previous lives."

"If that is true, please tell me what you know, Lord Buddha."

The Buddha began, "Many lives ago, there was an evil tyrant. He plundered and stole treasures from everywhere, using whatever despicable means he could. At that time, there was a general among the tyrant's advisors, who was blessed with kindness. The general had witnessed an incident in which a monk had angered the tyrant. The general stepped forward and protected the monk, convinving the tyrant to spare him. You were that general, and I was that monk."

"Now I understand!" The monk listened joyously. The Buddha's compassion relieved the monk's loneliness, healed his illness, and gave him back the warmth of community life and the joy of health.

The Buddha said, "Among the eight fields for cultivating merit, to tend to the sick is the greatest," The Buddha took this very seriously. Caring for the sick not only brings good luck, it is also a form of spiritual practice. As the Buddha's followers, we should aspire to be the doctors and nurses of all sentient beings.

The Joy of the Sangha

Among the earlier disciples of the Buddha, the Venerable Bhadra was the most respected. He frequently mentioned that leaving home to become a monk was his most joyous achievement.

The Buddha asked why he thought it such a joyous achievement.

Bhadra answered, "Lord Buddha, I used to live in a palace surrounded by an iron fence. Although warriors stood guard protecting me, I was still constantly in fear of being attacked or losing my life. Now, even though I am often alone in the forest meditating, I am happy and have no fear. The banquets, delicious food, and fancy clothes brought me no peace. Now, when I am in the forest I feel free and comfortable."

The Buddha answered happily, "I too, have had similar feelings."

The world of fame and wealth are truly a prison in which we are constantly in fear of losing our possessions. The sutras teach us to abandon fame and wealth to enjoy a carefree life.

Sakra-devanamindra and the Demon

Despite the fact that the Buddha always taught his disciples to be respectful and forgiving towards one other so that they could live together harmoniously and cultivate diligently, conflicts within the sangha still existed. One day, two monks had an argument which developed into a heated exchange of harsh words. When mediation by the others proved unsuccessful, the disagreement was reported to the Buddha. The Buddha took one look at the two red-faced monks involved in the incident, observed the rest of the disciples, and began to tell a story:

"Once there was a yaksa who was small, dark and extremely ugly. One day, this yaksa came to the heaven of the thirty-three and sat down on Sakra-devanamindra's throne.

At that moment, all the celestial beings in the heaven of the thirty-three were outraged by the daring behavior of the yaksa. They rebuked him bitterly without rest. Yet, as they shouted at him, the yaksa gradually grew taller and became better looking. When the celestial beings saw this they became even more furious, and the yaksa become even more stately and towering.

Not knowing how to deal with the situation, the celestial beings went to see Sakra-devanamindra and related the whole episode to him. Sakra-devanamindra thought, 'This yaksa must be extraordinary.' He went to the yaksa, faced him respectfully with joined palms and said three times, 'Virtuous one, I am Sakra-devanamindra, king of heaven of the thirty-three gods.'

Due to the humility of Sakra-devanamindra, the yaksa's arrogance grew, and as it grew, he became shorter and uglier until he disappeared altogether. Sakra-devanamindra ascended his throne and addressed all the celestial beings, 'From now on, never breed anger. When someone treats you with hostility, be cautious in your reaction. Do not add anger to anger. If someone offends you, do not offend that person in revenge. Treat that being with compassion instead. Always associate with those who have no anger or hostility, for they are the virtuous and sagely ones. Those who are easily angered are clouded by arrogance. When you become arrogant, you should control your emotions, just as you would control a fierce horse by its reins. This is the wholesome Dharma.'"

After the Buddha finished this story, he earnestly advised his disciples, "Although Sakra-devanamindra is in such a high position and enjoys such exceptional happiness, he is able to control his anger and praise others for their good temperament. You have joined the sangha and are cultivating the Way, should you not try even harder? All of you monks should learn from him."

Trying to stop anger by being angry is like pouring hot water onto a boil or adding oil to fire—you will never succeed. Only when the water of compassion is sprinkled upon it can the flame of anger be extinguished.

Protecting Rahula

During the time of the Buddha, the sangha had a rule about allowing only one person per room. More importantly, a novice monk had to respect and yield to an elder monk.

Once, the Venerable Rahula went to hear the Buddha teach the Dharma. While he was there, a monk from a distant land came to stay and was assigned to Rahula's room by the monk in charge of the dormitory. When Rahula returned from the day's teaching at sunset and discovered the arrangement, he dared not raise any questions as he had been taught by the Buddha to respect the elder monks and to practice patience. Seeing clouds gathering in the sky and realizing that a storm was coming, Rahula had nowhere to take cover but in the outhouse.

It did rain that night, and as the rain became heavier, the lowlands were flooded. A black snake from one of the holes nearby was forced to crawl out and it gradually made its way to the outhouse. Rahula's life was in danger. In his meditation, the Buddha suddenly thought of Rahula and knew he was in trouble. He immediately went to the outhouse and coughed once. He heard a cough from inside the outhouse in response.

The Buddha asked, "Who is in there?"

"It's me, Rahula."

"Come out, I need to talk to you."

When Rahula realized that it was the Buddha's voice, he quickly came out of the outhouse. Before he knew it, he was hugging the Buddha and sobbing. At this emotionally tender age, Rahula was still very fragile.

The Buddha asked Rahula why he was sleeping in the outhouse, and Rahula explained the situation to him. On hearing his story, the Buddha asked Rahula to take his own room instead.

Filled with delight, Rahula felt as if he had been delivered out of hell and into heaven.

The young children who leave their parents and loved ones to join the sangha really need the tender care of the older monks. This episode inspired the Buddha to establish a new rule that allowed novice monks to stay with a monk for two nights. The love of the Buddha was able to take care of even the slightest detail.

The Liberation of Nidhi

In ancient Indian society, the concept of occupational, hereditary, and ethnic differentiation gave rise to the caste system, which was comprised of four castes: Brahmans, who were religious leaders; Ksatriya, who were warriors and kings; Vaisya, who were merchants and artisans; and Sudra, who were farmers and laborers. It was generally accepted that the Sudras were born to serve as slaves. They received unfair treatment everywhere, and led extremely tragic lives.

This was true until the Buddha's awakening, when he revealed that "All sentient beings inherently possess the wisdom and nature of the Buddha." This implied absolute equality for all, that "When the four castes leave home and join the sangha, they all belong to the one clan of Sakyamuni." This was why that in the community of the Buddha, even the slighted Sudras could dwell among the others. Nidhi was a good example.

One day the Buddha and Ananda were begging for food in Sravasti. When they reached the outskirts of the city, they met Nidhi, whose work it was to dispose of human waste. Nidhi saw the Buddha from afar, and was very frightened. In his heart, he deeply admired the Buddha, but he thought he was too unworthy to see him. Nidhi felt that the pure and noble Buddha—a great teacher to all—should never be near someone like himself.

The Buddha knew of Nidhi's concerns. He sent Ananda back to the monastery and made his way to meet with Nidhi.

Seeing the Buddha approach him, Nidhi tried in vain to avoid the Buddha. In his attempts to hide, Nidhi accidentally turned over a pail of feces and the road was covered in filth. He was too terrified to know what to do, so he knelt down by the roadside. With his palms joined, he apologized, "Lord Buddha, I am so sorry!"

"Nidhi!" The Buddha called out his name.

Nidhi could not believe his ears. He thought, "Did the Buddha call out my name?" He could not even imagine such a thing. The Buddha once again said kindly, "Nidhi, will you come and join the sangha?"

Astonished, Nidhi replied, "Lord Buddha, I am a filthy and lowly person, would you really allow me to do that? All those in your sangha are either Sakyan princes or Brahmans. Could I too become one of your disciples?"

The Buddha said with a smile, "Nidhi, of course you can. The Dharma is like pure running water that can cleanse all filth. The Dharma is like a hot fire that can incinerate and destroy everything, be it large or small, good or bad. The Dharma is like the great sea that has the capacity to hold anything. When one accepts my teaching, one will leave all forms of desire behind. In my teaching, poverty, wealth, and caste are not an issue. They are illusory and unreal labels. The physical body is made up of the four elements and the five aggregates. Without wisdom and the commitment to practice, no one can be liberated."

Nidhi was filled with joy. He quietly followed the Buddha back to Jetavana Monastery. After they had arrived at the monastery, the Buddha told Ananda to take Nidhi down to the river to bathe him and then dress him in robes. The Buddha never abandoned any being. From this time forward, Nidhi never returned to his home life and became a disciple of the Buddha.

The Buddha's teachings are just like the vast ocean. The teachings are all encompassing and contain the spirit of compassion for all.

To Love and Care for Children

Among the ten great disciples of the Buddha, Katyayana was the greatest at debate. There was a time when he left the Buddha to go south to teach the Dharma in Rajagrha. One day, he sent one of his very young disciples back to Jetavana Monastery to see the Buddha. When the Buddha saw this young visitor who had traveled so far to see him, he immediately said to Ananda, "Ananda, Prepare an extra bed in my room for this little disciple of Katyayana to stay with me."

When the news of this kind gesture of the Buddha reached Katyayana, he was deeply impressed, and thereafter made additional effort to spread the Dharma. Witnessing how the Buddha cared for the young novice monk, his own disciples learned how to treat the novice monks in the sangha, such as Kunti and Rahula, with more care and dared not neglect them.

In the sutras, we often find the Buddha's sincere advice on how to respect those younger than us and not regard them as unimportant. Usually, the Buddha did not force rules onto his disciples. More often, he acted in accordance with what he taught and exemplified the Dharma through his own actions. This earned him great respect and wholehearted obedience from his followers, who came from all directions to learn from him.

The Folly of Not Forgiving Others

One day, when the Buddha returned from his alms rounds in Sravasti, he heard a lot of commotion. Upon inquiring, the Buddha found that two of his disciples had been involved in an argument. One of them angrily cursed the other while the latter remained silent. Moments later, the angry monk became aware of his wrongdoing and pleaded for forgiveness from the silent monk. However, the apology was not accepted by the silent one. In an attempt to resolve the conflict, the rest of the disciples tried to bring about an understanding between the two. This generated a lot of commotion in the monastery.

As soon as the Buddha learned of this incident, he said to them, "When one makes mistakes, it is much worse when one refuses to correct the mistakes. Once mistakes are found, as long as one has the courage to repent openly, one will regain peace and tranquility. It is just like how a dirty dusting cloth becomes clearn after it has been washed in water. When a person is willing to repent, one is still capable of learning. However, if a person refuses to accept others' genuine repentance, that person is foolish. That person will suffer the consequence of his hatred and will not receive any good fortune for a long time."

To elaborate his point further, the Buddha gave another analogy, "If one attempts to control the flame of an oil lamp by adding oil with a ladle, the flames will rage to the point of igniting the ladle itself. Hatred is the same. It is said that, 'Once the thought of hatred arises, the gates of thousands of obstacles are opened,' and, 'The fuel of hatred is capable of burning down an entire forest of merit.' Hatred in one's heart can destroy one's good karma, thereby bringing all kinds of obstacles to one's life.

Thus, a practitioner should guard against hatred. When one can cultivate one's mind and body, not only will there be benefit for oneself, but all sentient beings will be happy to be close to this person."

After hearing the Buddha's teaching, all his disciples became at ease with one another and the confrontation was resolved.

When one makes a mistake, one should have the courage and moral responsibility to repent and reform one's mistake. Such is the most courageous action. If others make mistakes, one should be forgiving and accept their apologies and repentance. This is the practice of compassion. It takes wisdom to correct one's mistakes and compassion to forgive others for their mistakes.

Part Seven:

The Monastic Life

The Buddha's sangha is an unparalleled field of merit for the world, made up of men and women who have chosen to search for the truth. It is said that monks and nuns leave the home life, but as they leave their homes they enter the world. They are our teachers, our friends, our brothers and sisters in the Dharma. They are our inspiration and our joy.

These stories are some of the Buddha's teachings to his monastics in celebration of that life, and teach us all how to become more content and carefree.

Sweeping the Floor of the Mind

One day as the Buddha approached the gate of Jetavana Monastery he saw a monk loudly sobbing. A crowd had gathered to laugh at and belittle him. The monk was named was Ksudrapanthaka, and he was not a very intelligent person. However, the Buddha knew that he was a righteous person. The Buddha thought highly of Ksudrapanthaka and had much compassion for him. When the Buddha saw the crowd, he asked Ksudrapanthaka, "Why are you crying?"

"Lord Buddha, I am such a stupid person! I left home with my brother to become a monk. Just now my brother was trying to teach me a verse, but I could not memorize the verse no matter how hard I tried. Eventually my brother said it was no use and that I shouldn't bother cultivating. He forbade me to stay here and told me to go home. When he asked me to leave, I started to cry. Oh, Lord Buddha, please have compassion and help me!"

After hearing this, the Buddha kindly consoled him and said, "Is this true? Do not worry, you may follow me and stay with me. Those who recognize their own ignorance are wise; it is ignorant people who think they are clever."

Upon returning to the monastery, the Buddha asked Ananda to teach Ksudrapanthaka. It was not long before Ananda also found it impossible to teach Ksudrapanthaka. Thus, the Buddha personally instructed Ksudrapanthaka. The Buddha taught him to recite the verse "Sweep and clean," but Ksudrapanthaka could not remember the verse. Everybody said that Ksudrapanthaka was hopeless. But the Buddha never gave up hope in any sentient being. The Buddha told Ksudrapanthaka, "Use the broom to sweep the floor, and dust the shoes, robes and sleeping mats of the other monks. While you sweep and dust, try to recite the verse."

Ksudrapanthaka followed the Buddha's advice and began serving the sangha by sweeping and dusting. The other monks became annoyed and forbade Ksudrapanthaka from sweeping and dusting their belongings. They found his sweeping and dusting a disturbance to their cultivation. The Buddha told the monks that Ksudrapanthaka was following his instructions, and that they were not to disturb his work.

Ksudrapanthaka took his work very seriously. By putting his mind fully behind learning the verse, he was finally able to remember "Sweep and clean." As time passed, he gradually began to understand the real meaning of the verse. He thought, "There are two kinds of dust: internal and external.. External dust is the sand and soil that is easily spotted and cleaned. Internal dust is the afflictions caused by the three poisons of greed, anger, and ignorance. This internal dust can only be cleaned by ultimate wisdom."

Ksudrapanthaka's mind slowly cleared and began to brighten. He was able to understand things he could not understand before. He thought, "Desire is like dust. A wise person must remove all desire. If desire is not removed, one cannot be free from the bonds of birth and death. This would be most pitiful. Desire is the cause of so much trouble and suffering. Desire is what keeps us from being free. Only when desire is gone can the mind be purified, free from bondage, and see the truth."

As Ksudrapanthaka thought this, he progressively extinguished the three poisons in his mind. He dwelled in a state of equanimity, neither desire nor hatred arose in him, and no good or bad thoughts were harbored in his mind. He was able to destroy the prison of delusion and his mind began to open up.

After Ksudrapanthaka was awakened, he joyfully went and bowed before the Buddha, "Lord Buddha, I now understand! I have swept away the dust from my mind!"

The Buddha was very happy. He praised Ksudrapanthaka, and told everyone, "If one studies the teachings but does not understand their profound meaning and does not put them into practice, then how can one benefit from it? By upholding and practicing just one verse, one is sure to attain awakening. Just look at the example of Ksudrapanthaka."

From then on, Ksudrapanthaka became well-known at Jetavana Monastery and was respected by everyone. However, Ksudrapanthaka's lifestyle did not change. Every day he continued to sweep the floor, and at each movement he whispered "sweep and clean."

Depending on the situation, the Buddha employs various methods to teach his disciples. The Buddha would never abandon any of his disciples. In the eyes of the Buddha, those without wisdom are like the seriously sick. With patience and compassion, there will be improvement. The Buddha is indeed the teacher of gods and humans, the greatest educator in the world.

Like Being Close to a Wonderful Fragrance

Once, there were more than seventy noble Brahman families living at the back of Vulture Peak, near the city of Rajagrha. Later, seventy men from those noble families ordained under the Buddha's teaching and entered the monastic life.

On one occasion, when the monks had still only recently been ordained, while traveling back to the monastery with the Buddha they became emotionally attached to their wives and families. They were very frustrated and started thinking about returning to the lay life.

Suddenly, the sky was covered with dark clouds and it began to rain heavily. At this moment, they became even more worried about their families. The Buddha could read their minds and knew their worries. He then used his supernatural power to alter many of the cottages along the road. The Buddha then led the monks into the cottages to seek shelter, but rain leaked into every one of them.

The Buddha analyzed the cause of the leaking to teach them: "If a house is not built well, it will leak when it rains. If the mind can not be focused on the right principle, then it will be disturbed by deviant views and sexual desire. However, if a house is built well, it will not leak when it rains. When the mind is able to be directed to the right principle, then it will not be invaded by deviant views and sexual desire." They listened to Buddha's teaching and roused themselves, but they were still very disheartened.

Meanwhile, the rain stopped, and the Buddha and his disciples continued their journey. On the way, they saw an old piece of paper on the ground. The Buddha asked one of the monks to pick it up, and asked "What kind of paper is this?"

The monk answered, "This paper was used to wrap incense. The fragrance has not vanished yet, even though it was discarded in an open field."

The Buddha continued, and soon saw a rope on the ground. The Buddha then asked another monk to pick it up, and asked him "What kind of rope is this?"

The monk answered, "This rope stinks! It was used to tie fish."

The Buddha told the monks, "The nature of sentient beings is pure. There are many different possible karmic effects resulting from different causes and conditions. One who befriends a virtuous person will have superior accomplishments and knowledge. One who befriends a vicious person will be stained black like one who is covered in ink, and be implicated in calamity. It is the same as your perceptions of the paper and the rope. The paper was fragrant and the rope stank. One who stays in a certain environment day after day will naturally be gradually influenced by it. As a result, one will no longer know right from wrong.

The Buddha then spoke in verse:

"Vulgarity is like being near a foul smell:
One becomes fascinated by bad habits and vices.
Virtue is like being near a fragrant smell:
One grows wise by learning virtuous deeds.
That person's behavior becomes fragrant and pure."

The Buddha advised the monks not to rigidly cling to their families. Doing so binds our minds with shackles so that we will never be free. Once again, they put their minds in the right place and were able to concentrate on their practice to achieve enlightenment.

The affection in the world makes for temporary happiness, but it comes with impurity and suffering. It is like the rope that was used to tie the fish. It will never be rid of the foul smell and the effect is the same for one's desires. When one stays near the Dharma, one will be influenced by virtuous desires. It is like the paper that was used to wrap the incense, the fragrance stays for a long time. That is the reason why one should strive to cultivate the Way.

Praying for the Impossible

On one occasion, the Venerable Gamini, when he had not been ordained for very long, asked the Buddha a question, "Lord Buddha, other religions believe that it is possible to pray one's way into heaven. Why don't you teach this? Wouldn't it be wonderful if you gave us the same teaching?"

The Buddha asked in return, "Gamini, is it possible for someone to throw a rock into a river and then pray to God to bring the rock to the surface of the water?"

Gamini replied, "Lord Buddha, that is impossible. How can a rock float on water?"

The Buddha said, "Correct. In the same way, it is impossible for someone who has accumulated unwholesome karma to enter heaven simply by praying to a god. The laws of nature is that whoever does unwholesome deeds falls into hell."

The Buddha continued, "Is it possible to pour oil into a river and then pray to a god to make the oil sink to the bottom?"

Gamini replied, "Lord Buddha, that is impossible. The oil would naturally rise to the surface of the water."

The Buddha said, "Correct. In the same way, no one can make someone who has performed wholesome actions fall into an unfortunate rebirth. By practicing wholesome actions, one naturally will enter heaven, while unwholesome actions will drag you into hell. This is the law of nature, and it cannot be altered simply by praying to a god."

After listening to the Buddha's teaching, Gamini never envied the practices of other religions.

The Harm of Offerings

There was a very large, peaceful forest near Sravasti. Because of its tranquility the Buddha would often take his disciples to the forest to practice. The Buddha named the forest, "The virtuous grove of renunciation."

As the burning hot summer came after a pleasant spring, the Buddha again led his disciples into the grove of renunciation. As soon as the villagers heard that the sangha had arrived in the forest, they came with many offerings. Before long, the entire forest was filled with offerings. Although the Buddha did not need offerings, they followed him wherever he went.

To prevent his disciples from being seduced by these offerings, the Buddha gathered all twelve thousand monks and taught them the harm in excessive offerings. The Buddha said, "Offerings are the biggest obstacle to cultivation. Even for someone who has attained the first level of enlightenment, the possibility of seduction is still there. Do not develop greed for offerings. Treat fame, offerings, and respect as a hindrance to cultivation. One should be detached from them all."

After listening to the Buddha's teaching, some of the monks were still confused. One such monk asked Buddha, "Lord Buddha, isn't it easier to attract people to listen to the teachings when famous? Isn't it easier to cultivate with offerings? Isn't it easier to sway people when one is respected? Why have you called offerings a hindrance to cultivation?"

The Buddha patiently explained, "Fame, offerings, and respect are obstructions to cultivation. They can severely damage your practice, peel the skin off your discipline, cut the flesh from your meditative concentration, break the bones of your wisdom, and suck the marrow out of your wholesome heart."

At this, one monk said, "Lord Buddha, if fame, offerings, and respect only bring destruction to people, we will be content with just these three robes and alms-bowl and live a simple, ascetic life."

Soon after this monk spoke, the other monks stood up and made the same vow. The Buddha saw their sincerity and joyfully praised them, "I am very happy that all of you enjoy the ascetic life. This is the Dharma of less desire, not more desire. This is the Dharma of being content, not discontent. This is the Dharma of peace, not agitation. This is the Dharma of diligence, not laziness. This is the Dharma of correct thinking, not false thinking. This is the Dharma of concentration, not idle wandering. This is the Dharma of wisdom, not ignorance."

The monks gladly accepted the Buddha's advice after hearing his teachings. Soon afterwards, many of them became awakened.

With the dramatic change of social structure, Buddhist practice is no longer kept only in the mountains and monasteries.

It is has spread throughout society to benefit others. In order to spread the teachings within society, a teacher must first cultivate himself. Only then can he benefit others.

Sariputra's Shadow

One sunny day, while the Buddha and Sariputra were standing together in a courtyard, a dove landed in Sariputra's shadow. While resting there, the dove shivered and remained extremely apprehensive, constantly casting a nervous gaze around the courtyard. In a little while, the dove flew off and alighted within the Buddha's shadow. Immediately, the bird became extraordinarily peaceful and calm, as if it had found a nice shelter. Upon witnessing this phenomenon, Sariputra asked the Buddha with curiosity, "I had no intention of killing the dove, why was it so tense when it was near me?"

The Buddha replied, "Although you lacked the specific thought of killing the bird, it still felt the residual, habitual anger lingering inside of you."

Ashamed, Sariputra said, "My Lord Buddha, I understand. From now on I will cultivate compassion. If a bird will not come near me without fear, how can I guide others to awakening?"

Bad habits are behaviors we have become accustomed to and conceal from others. They are residues from the accumulation of our worries. In the sutras, bad habits are described as seeds that are planted in our mind. Whenever they meet the right cause they sprout and result in unwholesome deeds. We have been carrying the residue of greed, anger and delusion through all our lifetimes.

To practice the Dharma is to remove bad seeds and replace them with good ones. We often hear that old habits are hard to break. There is a similar Chinese saying that goes, "Destroying a mountain or changing the course of a river is easy. Changing one's habits is difficult."

Being difficult does not imply that it can never be done. As long as we are determined and repent our previous bad actions, we will surely achieve our goals. The Buddha taught us that all beings have Buddha nature. If everyone can become a Buddha, what is there that cannot be accomplished?

The Six Contemplations

One day, the Buddha's half brother, Mahanama, asked the Buddha "You often tell us that only boundless, supreme nirvana is ultimate happiness. How can we reach supreme nirvana?"

The Buddha replied, "In order to reach nirvana, you must practice the six contemplations. Just as a starving man requires nutritious food to revive his body, you must practice the six contemplations to reach nirvana."

"What are the six contemplations?" Mahanama asked.

The Buddha began to explain, "First is contemplation of the Buddha. One should often chant the Buddha's name and focus on the wisdom, light, and power of the Buddha. One should take refuge in the Buddha."

"Second is contemplation of the Dharma. Study the sutras and the higher teachings. These are my authoritative teachings. The Dharma is the truth that leads to liberation, so cultivate and practice accordingly.

"Third is contemplation of the sangha. The sangha is the

community of those who maintain and pass on the Buddha's great wisdom to eradicate delusion. The sangha upholds teachings on discipline, meditative concentration, and wisdom, and are a field of merit for this world. To properly cultivate, one should respect the sangha as a body of teachers.

"Fourth is contemplation of the precepts. One should observe the five precepts to stem injustice and put an end to unwholesome action, speech, and thought.

"Fifth is contemplation of generosity. One can eliminate greed and stinginess by giving. It is only through generosity that we can accrue merit.

"Sixth is contemplation of the benefit of being reborn in heaven. In heaven, one is endlessly happy. One should cultivate and do good deeds to ensure a rebirth in heaven."

Four Kinds of Disciples

As the Buddha's teaching began to spread far and wide, the Buddha gained many new disciples. As the sangha grew, its new members were of greatly varying faculties. Just as fingers do not grow to the same length and even the most closely attended fields grow weeds, some members of the sangha no longer quickly attained awakening.

One day, when the Buddha was explaining the Dharma to his disciples, one stood up and asked, "Lord Buddha, could you tell us what are the characteristics of an ideal disciple?"

"Good question," the Buddha answered, "My disciples are like the four kinds of birds. There are birds that have a beautiful body but an ugly voice, birds that have an ugly body but a beautiful voice, birds that have an ugly body and an ugly voice, and birds that have a beautiful body and a beautiful voice."

"Just as there are four kinds of birds, there are four kinds of practitioners. One from the first group of practitioners has a fine appearance but does not practice well nor study the sutras.

"One from the second group of practitioners has an inferior appearance, but he studies the sutras diligently. He fully understand the Dharma and observe the precepts. His actions are complete.

"One from the third group of practitioners hardly follows the teachings at all. He is lazy, careless and lacks deep faith in the Dharma. Subsequently, he falls into wrong views.

"One from the fourth group of practitioners not only has a solemn appearance but he also diligently studies the sutras. He practice diligently and observes the precepts. Even when he commits some slight fault, he immediately repents and reforms his behavior, to say nothing of when he makes big mistakes. He abides by the Dharma and knows every verse by heart.

"You should all look up to those in the fourth group of practitioners. They are my ideal disciples. I hope you can contemplate and learn from this."

After the Buddha had spoken, all his disciples gladly followed his teachings.

The Seven Carriages

During the rainy season, the Buddha came to Rajagrha to teach the Dharma and settled with his disciples in the Bamboo Grove for the rains retreat. At that time, the Venerable Purna was among the monks. At the end of the three-month retreat, the Buddha asked all the monks, "Where is your place of origin?

Why did you come here for the rains retreat?"

Each monk responded in turn by saying where he had grown up, and that he had come to the rains retreat to attain the joy of liberation and eternal bliss.

"Monks, if that is the case, can you all be content? Can you all diligently pursue the truth? Can you all practice with determination, right mindfulness, and a joyful heart?" The Buddha raised a series of questions.

"Yes, we can, Lord Buddha," each monk responded, "After this retreat, we all feel peaceful and free in our bodies and minds, and experience unparalleled bliss and joy in the Dharma."

"This is only one stage in your spiritual practice. These experiences cannot be called awakening."

While in deep meditation, the Buddha realized that Purna had awakened during the retreat. The Buddha turned to him and said, "Purna, do not hesitate to share what you gained during the three-month retreat with us."

"Yes, Lord Buddha. I, your disciple, started by contemplating my mind. I then cleansed my mind of all lustful and desirous influences. Lastly, I practiced self-contentment. Diligently pursuing the stages in the proper order, I practiced right mindfulness until I attained one-pointed concentration. I beheld truth with a pure mind and attained the happiness of liberation."

"Monks, Purna speaks truly. Once, King Prasenajit had to travel from Sravasti to a city north of Kausala to listen to the Dharma. To get there on time, he changed carriages seven times in one day. Using his wisdom King Prasenajit traveled quickly and arrived in time to hear the teachings. One must use correct method in order to achieve one's goals."

After they heard the Buddha's instructions, the monks realized that they could not only be diligent, but had to apply the correct method in order to practice well. They once again followed the instructions on the proper order of practice, and many eventually attained awakening.

Spiritual practice requires the application of persistence and perseverance, but it also requires observing correct procedure. Spiritual goals cannot be attained instantaneously or with little practice. Even the Buddha, with all his sagely qualities, practiced asceticism for six years. King Prasenajit, too, with all his worldly wisdom, went through seven transfers of carriages in order to listen to the Dharma. To hear the Dharma is rare indeed. In order not to squander such a good opportunity, one must not be negligent or disrespectful.

What is Happiness?

On one occasion, four newly ordained monks were sitting together under a tree meditating. The tree was so tall that it reached up to the clouds, and its numerous thick branches were full of luxuriant foliage. The blossoms of the tree gave off a pleasant fragrance, which wafted down to the monks below. The environment brought out the four monks' interest in the wordly life, so after their meditation, they began to discuss the loveliest things in this world of abundance, and what brings the most happiness to people.

The first one said, "People receive the most happiness when all the flowers are blooming in spring and they are out in the countryside enjoying a picnic."

The second one said, "People receive the most happiness when they can attend banquets hosted by their friends and relatives where they can drink wine, socialize, sing, and dance."

The third one said, "People receive the most happiness when they have abundant wealth and own chariots, fashionable clothing, and accessories so they can stand out in a crowd and come and go in glory."

The fourth one said, "People receive the most happiness when they have beautiful wives and concubines dressed in extravagant clothes and wearing alluring perfume with which they can enjoy the pleasures of life."

The Buddha noticed that the four monks were deep in discussion, so he approach them and asked, "What topic were you discussing under this tree?"

They saw that the Buddha was upon them, and they stood up at once to greet him, each relating what they considered the happiest situation in the world.

The Buddha responded to them, "The examples you gave lead to the worries of human society. They do not last."

The Buddha continued, "Nature flourishes in spring and summer, but decays in autumn and winter. The happy gathering of friends and relative merely precedes the inevitable farewell and separation. Wealth and wordly possessions cannot withstand floods, fire, thieves, and tyranny. Beautiful wives bring misfortunes arising from love and hatred. Therefore, an ordinary person born in this world constantly brings disaster and ill-will with each move he makes, breaking his family and costing him his life.

"In this world there is endless sorrow and fear of the three lower realms and the eight difficulties. Nothing can be controlled by human wishes. Monks, your hearts must remain pure and you must not chase after external things. Do not seek fame and wealth; concentrate on your practice. Only then can you walk the path that leads to nirvana. This alone leads to true happiness."

The Buddha's lecture helped the monks to realize their mistake. Ashamed, they resolved to calm their affliction and to practice diligently.

Though worldly enjoyment can bring us a moment of happiness, it ultimately transforms into pain. Worldly happiness is short and ever-changing. If we pursue it, it may even cost us our lives. One must be wary.

The Eight Virtues of a Good Horse

One day the Buddha saw a tame horse moving to the instructions of a horse-trainer in the city of Sravasti. The Buddha went up to the horse and said, "This is an excellent horse."

"True," replied the horse-trainer, and he proceeded to expound the characteristics of a good horse. The Buddha listened closely, nodded his head in agreement, and patted the horse on the back. After that, the Buddha went directly back to the Bamboo Grove.

That evening, the Buddha asked his disciples what the characteristics of a good horse were. His disciples looked at the Buddha with surprise, wondering why he brought up such a subject.

Noticing that his disciples were confused, the Buddha said, "Good horses have eight virtues: First, they are submissive and do not scare people. Second, they are not picky about their feed. Third, they rest in a clean place. Fourth, they follow the instructions of their trainer. Fifth, they are used to pulling chariots, and work hard at it. Sixth, they know the right path and avoid the wrong path. Seventh, even if they are sick or old, they do their best when pulling a chariot. Eighth, they are never tired or lazy."

The Buddha continued, "A saint also has eight virtues: First, he follows the laws of the land and protects morality. Second, he brings joy to others and does not frighten them. Third, he treats others with equality. Fourth, he is restrained from unwholesome actions, speech, and thoughts, and does not hold false views. Fifth, he does not conceal his own wrongdoing and ends bad habits as soon as he becomes aware of them. Sixth, he studies diligently and fulfills his vows with care. Seventh, he is open and does nothing that he would be ashamed of later. Eight, he is not lazy but diligent and enthusiastic."

After having heard this, the discples all accepted the Buddha's teaching and practiced diligently.

Eight Characteristics of a Bad Horse

In the city of Rajagrha there was a market that was always noisy and exciting and full of people. One day the Buddha led his disciples into this market.

"I have all kinds of horses!" shouted one of the horse traders, "You'll surely find one you'll like no matter what you're looking for!"

The Buddha and his disciples watched as people traded horses. One monk could not help but mention how gentle the horses looked. "You are right," another monk commented, "Trained horses are astounding."

Once they had returned to the Bamboo Grove, the Buddha

asked his disciples, "What is an untrained horse like?"

One person stood up and answered, "Untrained horses are wild. They will attack anyone who approaches them."

"A bad horse has eight characteristics," the Buddha said in response, "First, they will knock over their chariot. Second, their chariots speed out of control. Third, they make their chariots spin. Fourth, they do not move when they are told to do so. Fifth, they lead their chariots to crash into one another. Sixth, they do not have a good sense of direction. Seventh, they harm their owners. Eighth, they try to break loose of their chariots."

After the Buddha finished speaking, the disciples felt surprised that a horse could be so different from the trained horses they had seen earlier that morning.

The Buddha then looked at them solemnly and said, "Wicked people are just like bad horses. When their wrongdoing is uncovered, they have eight characteristics. First, they become angry. Second, they fight back with foul language. Third, they become filled with hatred. Fourth, they do not admit their faults and repent. Fifth, they turn away. Sixth, they will not answer any questions. Seventh, they will argue with anyone who tries to mediate. Eighth, they try to cover up their wrongdoing. Those who have these eight traits are just like bad horses. No one wants to deal with wicked people just as no one wants to have bad horses."

A Secluded Valley

Once, while the Buddha was teaching the Dharma at Vulture Peak to the celestial beings, a brave and courageous monk expressed a desire to put more effort into his practice. The

Buddha directed him to a valley and instructed him to sit under a tree and practice breathing meditation.

Although it was very quiet down in the valley, the monk would occasionally hear conversations, though he could see no signs of anyone speaking. This sent a chill down his spine and he was unable to settle down and concentrate on meditation. This greatly troubled him, and he mumbled to himself, "I am from a noble family. I have left home to be a monk and find peace. Yet, here I am all by myself, without companions, haunted by ghosts. I still cannot find peace. I might as well go home."

Still troubled, the Buddha arrived and sat down next to him and asked, "Are you afraid of being alone?"

After bowing to the Buddha, the monk answered, "I never lived in the woods before. Now that I am here all by myself, I do feel a bit afraid."

At that moment, an enormous wild elephant walked toward a large tree that was nearby and lay down next to it, enjoying the joy of being away from others. The Buddha knew the thoughts of this elephant, and asked the monk, "Do you know where this elephant came from?"

"I have no idea," replied the monk.

The Buddha told him, "This elephant is from a herd of about five hundred. He left them behind in order to sleep soundly under that tree. He understands the joy of leaving the bonds of family life. Elephants are animals, yet they also hope to find peace. You have become a monk and taken a vow to practice no matter what, yet you still feel lonely and in need of a companion. A companion would only be an obstacle to your practice. It is best for you to cultivate alone."

After listening to the Buddha's teaching, the monk understood and practiced peacefully. The ghosts that had haunted him also took the teachings to heart and ceased disturbing the monk.

Practice is about relinquishing your inner fears, desires, and foolish thoughts; it is not just a matter of staying away from people.

Matanga's Conversion

Among the Buddha's monastic followers, Ananda was the youngest and the best looking. His face was as glorious as the full moon, and his eyes were as pure as lotus blossoms. He was also very intelligent. Once he heard the Buddha's words, he would never forget them.

Once, when Ananda was on his way back from collecting alms, he came across a young servant girl named Matanga. Ananda was thirsty, so he asked her for some water.

Matanga was very pleased, and respectfully offered Ananda water with both her hands. Ananda did not regard her with any contempt, but politely thanked her with a nod. Matanga was very grateful for his gesture, and was enchanted by Ananda's charm and elegance. After Anada finished drinking and left, she gazed at him as he walked away, and her heart filled with love and admiration for him.

From that time on, Matanga used many ways to lure Ananda. When Ananda would come out from Jetavana Monastery, Matanga would be overjoyed and she would follow close behind him. Even when Ananda wanted to distance himself, she would still keep very close by. Ananda thought she was shameless, and often returned to the monastery before collecting enough alms.

The rains retreat was set to start soon, during which the Buddha and his disciples would not leave the monastery. Matanga anxiously waited the three months for the retreat to end, and when Ananda emerged again to collect alms, she followed right behind him. Ananda felt helpless. When he returned to the monastery, he knelt in front of the Buddha and said, "Lord Buddha, a woman named Matanga is trying to seduce me. She follows me everywhere I go. Lord Buddha, please kindly help me get away from her."

The Buddha smiled and said, "Ananda, why does a woman render you helpless? This is because you have too heavily emphasized listening and learning and have not sufficiently emphasized practice and upholding precepts. Once confronted by seduction, you feel too weak to resist. Do not worry, I can help you. If you follow my advice you should never run into such trouble again." The Buddha then told Ananda to bring Matanga to him.

Ananda went out as ordered and saw Matanga still wandering outside the front door. Ananda then walked up to her and asked, "Why do you always follow me around?"

On hearing this, Matanga was overjoyed and replied, "You are such a fool, why would you ask such a question? When you first asked me for water, your words were so gentle and sweet, and you treated me so kindly and lovingly. I was willing to give you all of my heart, but you ran away without a word. You and I are both young and attractive. I want you to enjoy life's pleasures with me. Even if the oceans dry up and the mountains crumble, my love for you will never change."

Ananda replied somewhat shyly, "My teacher, the Buddha, would like to see you. Come with me and the Buddha will decide what is right for me." Matanga hesitated, but when she heard that the Buddha would make a decision, she mustered her courage and overcame her shame. She went with Ananda to where the Buddha was residing.

"Do you wish to marry Ananda?" the Buddha asked her directly.

"Yes." Matanga replied with her hands in front of her chest and her head bowed.

"Marriage between a man and a woman requires the permission of the parents. Can you ask your parents to come here to discuss it?"

"My parents have given their permission, and my mother has also met Ananda. If you do not believe it, I can go home right now and bring my mother here."

Matanga went home and brought her mother to Jetavana Monastery. When she returned she bowed to the Buddha and said, "Lord Buddha, my mother is here to pay homage to you." The Buddha then asked her mother, "Have you given your consent for your daughter to marry Ananda? Since Ananda is a monk, you should let your daughter become a nun and then she may marry Ananda. Do you agree?"

Matanga's mother replied, "It is all right with me. I would be very pleased with this."

The Buddha then ordered, "You may now return home and your daughter will remain with us."

After her mother left, the Buddha said to Matanga, "Since you are to marry Ananda, you must first become a nun and practice diligently. When your practice is as cultivated as Ananda's, then I will conduct the wedding ceremony for you."

Matanga was all set to become Ananda's wife, and she happily shaved her head and dyed her robes. She wholeheartedly listened to the Buddha's teachings and diligently practiced, as instructed by the Buddha. She lived the life according to the teachings in the monastic community just like the rest of the sangha.

Matanga's mind became more calm day by day. She then realized that her attachment to love in the past was actually despicable behavior. The Buddha often taught that the impurities of the five desires were the source of all suffering. Only the foolish moth would plunge into the fire to be burnt. The ignorant silkworm would weave its cocoon and be bound. The desires for the five senses must be eliminated before the mind can be purified and life can be peaceful.

Eventually, Matanga realized her obsession with Ananda was disrespectful. One day, with tears running down her face, she knelt in front of Buddha and repented, "Great Buddha, I have now completely awakened from my foolish dreams. I shall no longer behave as foolishly as I did. I understand that what I have now attained may even surpass the attainment of the monk, Ananda. I am very grateful to you, Lord Buddha. In order to teach ignorant beings such as us, you use all kinds of skillful means. Lord Buddha, please have mercy on me and allow me to repent. I will always follow your footsteps and walk towards the truth. I will obey your teachings and be a teacher of the truth."

The Buddha smiled with satisfaction and replied, "Very good, Matanga! I knew that you would attain your present state of cultivation. You are very intelligent. From now on I do not have to worry about you. I am very happy for you."

The wonderful story of Matanga's conversion became a legend in the monastic community.

The Body is The Root of Misery

One day, four recently ordained monks were cultivating under a big tree, and were discussing the most distressful parts of human life. One of them expressed his opinion, "The most distressful part of human life is sexual passion. If the lust for sex cannot be put away, there will be no way to enter the path to awakening."

Another said, "The most distressful part of human life is the desire for food and drink. Nothing can be done if one faces hunger and thirst."

The third monk came up with an idea, "I think that anger is the most distressful part of human life. If there is even a single angry thought in one's mind, countless hindrances appear during cultivation. Anger will cause a person to suffer through infinite negative karmic effects."

The last one added, "Terror and fear are the most distressful part of human life. No one can live a peaceful life if one faces terror and fear every day."

The Buddha then came by and asked them what the topic of their lively discussion was. The four monks reported their ideas respectively. Afterwards the Buddha corrected them and said, "It is a joy and an aide to cultivation to have frequent meetings to discuss your views on your practice. However, although there are valid points in each of your statements, they have yet to reach the heart of the issue.

"All the suffering and anguish in the world stems from the body which is composed of the five aggregates. The body is the root of all misery and grief. We call this body the instrument of pain. It is through the body that we feel hunger, thirst, cold, warmth, trouble, terror, desire and unwholesome intentions. It is because of this body that sentient beings experience toil, worry, grief, fear, and death in the endless cycle of birth and death within the six realms.

"In order to get rid of this worldly suffering, you must achieve tranquility. This is the true end of suffering. Calm desire, extinguish the fire of anger, and face this world of illusions with an attitude that is serene and imperturbable. As time goes by, tranquility will emerge."

After hearing the Buddha's teachings, the four monks became humble and practiced diligently, and quickly realized the attainment of their cultivation.

Why One Joins the Sangha

One of the deepest regrets of the Buddha was Devadatta's betrayal. Not only did he leave the Buddha, but he also used the offerings of King Ajatasatru to tempt the Buddha's other disciples into following him. A small number of those disciples who were not strong in their faith and lacked will power could not resist the bribery of Devadatta. They defected from the Buddha and supported Devadatta instead.

However, the Buddha was not at all upset over this defection. With a calm composure, he told his disciples, "When the center of a banana hardens, its death is not far away; when a mule is pregnant, it will soon die; if a person receives too many offerings or experiences too much material enjoyment, his cultivation will easily deteriorate, and failure will soon be at hand."

A few days later, the Venerable Sariputra came to the

community of Devadatta. With his solemn and irrefutable eloquence, he addressed the followers of Devadatta and the defected disciples of the Buddha, "I wish to ask all of you, did you join the sangha to receive offerings or are you here to cultivate?"

All of the disciples answered, "We are here to cultivate and escape from the cycle of birth and death in this sea of suffering."

"If this is the case, why are you not practicing the correct path of the Buddha? Why do you allow your practice of pure and noble beliefs to be shaken by material offerings? You should repent your past actions and reform without delay!"

As Sariputra said this, countless rays of golden light shone from all over his body. In the midst of these rays appeared the kind countenance of the Buddha. The disciples who had defected and the supporters of Devadatta all knelt down to repent at the sight of this, and Sariputra led them back to the sangha. When the Buddha saw these disciples who had previously left he felt neither anger nor joy, but simply said calmly, "You only have to turn back, and the far shore is within reach. Let us work hard and never be lax in our cultivation."

The Buddha does not abandon anyone, not even those who are stubborn and deluded. Instead he embraces them with compassion. He does not use authority or violence to pressure them into submission because this would only result in a superficial surrender. The Buddha has established himself as a noble example, as pure and clear as the moon and as refreshing as a light breeze. He is innately respected by all for his morality and supremely virtuous character, and his leadership is gratefully and confidently accepted by all sentient beings.

Balance in Collecting Alms

After the Buddha attained awakening, all his daily activities were either beneficial for himself or others. To benefit himself he would meditate, by which he could attain samadhi and enjoy the bliss of the Dharma. To benefit others, he taught the Dharma to the sangha, spread his teaching, and collected alms. Collecting alms in particular drew people to the Buddha and his followers, which gave him the opportunity to teach the Dharma and benefit others. The *Diamond Sutra* describes the Buddha's daily routine well: "At that time, it was mealtime for the World-Honored One. He put on his robe, and with a bowl in hand, entered the city to collect alms from one household to the next."

"Collecting alms from one household to the next" implies that he would collect alms from both the rich and the poor without discrimination. Nevertheless, among the ten great discples of the Buddha, the Venerable Mahakasyapa, who was well known for his adherence to ascetic practices, never collected alms from the rich. His reasoning was that those who were rich already must have accumulated merit in their past lives through their generosity. Why should he bother to allow those who already had great merit to gain even more merit? Instead, he thought that he should direct his attention to helping the poor by providing them with the opportunity to gain merit. Thus he would only collect alms from the poor, never from the rich.

On the other hand, the Venerbale Subhuti, who was well known for his wisdom of emptiness, did just the reverse. He felt that the poor could not even cope with their own basic provisions for a decent living, and he was not willing to add to their burden by collecting alms from them. For the rich, giving away a portion of their belongings would have a minimal impact on their level of comfort; so he would only collect alms from the rich, never from the poor.

Mahakasyapa's and Subhuti's two extremes came to the Buddha's attention, and he called for an assembly to advise them, "Collecting alms from only the rich or the poor is unbalanced. My teachings are based upon equality. Although this world is full of differentiation and unequal treatment, we should commit ourselves to equality. This will be a great benefit to both others and ourselves."

An unbalanced mind is the basic cause of controversy in modern society. When one breeds comparison, one starts to be calculating, and controversy will follow. Although everyone wants to be treated fairly, in reality, there is no absolute fairness. It is true that we are all equal in our Buddha nature. However, events differ because of our different causes and conditions.

From the past to the present, we have created a myriad of different karma. Everyone's merit and past karma is different, therefore, the results encountered are naturally different. When we observe what goes on in the world, we think the world cannot possibly be fair. We can only maintain a balance in how we see things in our minds. If each one of us can truly understand karma and the Law of Cause and Effect, we can elevate our views to see beyond worldly injustice.

If everyone sees things in this way, all people can live in harmony. This state is described well in the Platform Sutra of the Sixth Patriarch: *"With an even mind, why bother upholding precepts? With an upright practice, why meditate?"*

PART EIGHT:

LAY TEACHINGS

The Buddha did not only teach us how to sit and meditate, he taught the Truth— the truth of the family, the truth of politics, the truth of wealth. The Buddha taught the truth of life.

Buddhism is about transforming greed into generosity, anger into loving-kindness and compassion, and ignorance into wisdom. These are not distant intangible ideals, but affect us every day. These stories are the Buddha's teachings to some of his lay followers, and show us how we can be more giving, loving, and wise in our everyday lives.

Sujata Becomes a Follower of Buddha

Near Magadha, along the banks of the Ganges River, there was a young man from a wealthy family who would come to the countryside each morning. He would then wet his clothes and hair, join his palms, and bow in the direction of the east, south, west, north, zenith, and nadir.

One day the Buddha ran into this young man on his way to his daily ritual. The Buddha came forward and kindly asked him "Good man, what is your name? Why have you come to the countryside this morning, wet yourself, and paid homage to each direction?"

The young man looked at the Buddha in surprise "Oh! Lord Buddha, I have heard much about you, though I have never had the chance to hear your teachings in person. My name is Sujata. Before he died, my father told me to honor each of the six directions every day. I do this to remember and honor him."

The Buddha said kindly and solemnly "Sujata, you only honor the six directions physically. Considering the vastness and emptiness of the universe, it doesn't mean a thing. In my sagely teachings, we also honor the six directions, but not the six directions you honor."

Sujata replied, confused, "What are the six directions in your sagely teachings? Please instruct me."

The Buddha replied, "Sujata, in my teachings, these are six directions people have to pay respect to:

(1) "Parents are represented by the east. Children should honor their parents in these five ways: by caring fortheir material needs, by informing them of major decisions, by respecting what

they do, by following and obeying what they righteously ask of you, and by continuing their right livelihood and practicing generosity after their death.

"Parents should honor their children in these five ways: by properly educating them so that they follow the right path, by reminding them of their virtues and making them act with integrity, by kindly educating them so they are knowledgeable, by finding them decent spouses, and by providing for them what they need to succeed in their careers.

(2) Teachers are represented by the south. Students should honor their teachers in these five ways: by standing up when they approach to show respect, by providing for them and receiving their teachings compliantly, by doing as they ask of you, by carefully following their instructions, and by not forgetting what they teach you.

Teachers should honor their students in these fives ways: by instructing and guiding them with loving-kindness, by teaching them what they do not know, by answering their questions and making sure they understand, by introducing them to good people to ensure they have decent company, and by teaching them all that is known without holding back.

(3) Spouses are represented by the west. Husbands should honor their wives in these five ways: by treating them with courtesy and respect, by being loyal and trustworthy, by caring for their needs, by being considerate and passionate, and by delegating the decisions of the house to them.

Wives should honor their husbands in these five ways: by arising first and cleaning the house each morning, by allowing them to sit first at a meal, by being kind and not using rough language, by following their will and not going against them, and by consulting their opinion before a major undertaking.

(4) Relatives and friends are represented by the north. You should honor your friends and relatives in these five ways: by helping them when they are in need, by speaking kindly and respectfully to them, by sharing one's gains and being fair, by helping them through difficulties, and by being honest and never cheating them.

Friends and relatives should honor you in these five ways: by encouraging you and not allowing you to indulge in improper conduct, by advising you not to waste your money, by making you feel courageous and not intimidated, by privately advising you to set you on the right track, and by constantly praising your good deeds and never mentioning your wrongdoings.

(5) Servants are represented by the nadir. Masters should honor their servants in these fives ways: by not overworking them, by feeding them well, by having them work regular hours, by caring for their illnesses, and by giving them surplus goods.

Servants should honor their masters in these fives ways: by getting up early and working diligently, by being responsible and not being indifferent towards work, by being loyal to them and not taking what is theirs, by working enthusiastically and finishing the work one step at a time, and by praising them and their good deeds.

(6) Monastics are represented by the zenith. Laypeople should honor monastics in these five ways: by being kind and not killing or stealing, by always encouraging others and avoiding lying, by mindfully helping others and not being greedy or

angry, by providing for them, and by allowing them into your home.

Monastics should honor laypeople in these five ways: by mindfully observing their actions and ensuring they do not commit wrongdoings, by showing them good deeds and encouraging them to do more, by always being kind and never having evil thoughts, by ensuring that they have right view and that they understand the meaning of what is learned, and by constantly speaking of the way to liberation.

"Sujata, if you honor these six sagely directions then you will always act properly, your will turn away from ignorance and stubbornness, and you will work hard and diligently on the right path. You will also have many good, moral, and knowledgeable friends. Always pay attention to how to help others. Vow to cultivate the four immeasurable minds: kindness, compassion, joy, and equanimity. Always use your speech to comfort others. This is the way to remember and honor your father."

After having heard all this, Sujata suddenly found profound wisdom. He was overwhelmed with joy and vowed to practice what the Buddha had taught him for the rest of his life. He immediately became a follower of the Buddha, gave up his foolish worship of the six physical directions, and took refuge in the Triple Gem.

Cultivation lies in diligent practice, not formalities. The Buddha taught Sujata to respect parents, teachers, spouses, relatives, servants, and monastics. From this we can see that the Buddha recognized the ways of the world, and we can appreciate the Buddha's emphasis on the practice of Buddhism in everyday life.

Four Ways to Attain Happiness

Once, a devoted lay follower asked the Buddha, "Lord Buddha, how does a lay person attain happiness in this life?"

The Buddha told him, "A lay person can attain happiness by doing four things."

"What are these four things?" the lay disciple asked.

The Buddha said, "First, perfect your livelihood. Whether you are a farmer, a laborer, a merchant, a teacher, or whatever your occupation, you should rely on a proper skill and earn a proper living.

"Second, perfect your savings. Excluding the usual daily necessities and expenses, you should save your earnings to avoid loss.

"Third, perfect your friendships. You should befriend virtuous people and avoid befriending people who are insincere or vicious.

"Fourth, perfect your standard of living. You should not waste your fortunes. Do not be overly stingy, but have a reasonable standard of living."

After listening to Buddha's advice on the four ways to attaining happiness, the lay follower praised the teaching as if she had just received a rare treasure.

Eight Realizatins of a Bodhisattva

One day, while Aniruddha was meditating in a country village, he thought, "The Way cannot be attained through greed, but only through contentment. The Way cannot be sought in a noisy place, but only in tranquility. It takes diligence, right mindfulness, a great deal of knowledge and wisdom to find the Way."

The Buddha was residing at Deer Park at that time and knew Aniruddha was thinking this, so he made a special trip to the village to praise Aniruddha. Aniruddha, happy to see his teacher said, "Lord Buddha, in the sangha, with its six points of reverent harmony, we all know not to emphasize the self. But, Lord Buddha, what about those many followers who have not left the household life, or those who stay close to society in order to teach the Dharma and benefit people? How can they attain awakening and nirvana? Please teach us."

"Aniruddha, you have asked a very good question. I will now teach you the eight realizations of a bodhisattva. All my disciples should memorize the following: existance.

"First, know that the world and life are impermanent, full of suffering, empty, impure, and do not have a true self. One must examine them in this way to attain awakening.

"Second, know that the origin of suffering is greed for worldly things. Removing desire and freeing oneself from the passions of the senses is the way to free your body and mind.

"Third, look into the mind and be dissatisfied with desire. Desire drives us to greed and creates unwholesome actions. If one can dwell in poverty, be happy and content, and pursue wisdom, this is the way to have a stable life.

"Fourth, do not be lazy in doing good. Do not be disappointed by the affairs that benefit worldly people. Putting an end to one's worries and stopping what is unwholesome is the way to exit the prison of the three realms.

"Fifth, see the terror in the cycle of birth and death. Diligently study the teachings. After you have mastered them, become determined to teach all sentient beings and give them happiness.

"Sixth, realize that those who are poor often complain and feel hatred. A bodhisattva should give charity and comfort and advice them to end their hatred and complaints.

"Seventh, do not be defeated by the five worldly desires. Whether or not one has left the household life, do not be attached to worldly pleasure. Maintain a tranquil and upright mind.

"Eighth, do not only be concerned with caring for oneself. Initiate the Mahayana mind of benefitting and helping all beings. One must see that all sentient beings are free from suffering before making an effort for one's own wellness."

The Buddha taught these eight realizations of a bodhisattva that lead to Buddhahood in response to Aniruddha's question. Many people have since followed this way and have vastly improved their lives. They have gained the happiness of self-dependency.

For the Protection of the Dharma

Once, the Buddha was in Rajagrha teaching the fourteen right practices to sixteen kings, including King Prasenajit.

The Buddha told the kings, "Whenever there are disasters in your countries, you should build one hundred altars and invite one hundred monks to recite the Sutra on the Prajnaparamita of the Benevolent King twice a day. Countless ghosts and spirits will listen to the recitation and come to protect your countries. In this way, all disasters and calamities will be annihilated."

Meanwhile, the Buddha said to King Prasenajit, "After I have entered parinirvana, when the Dharma has diminished to the point where it no longer is present, there will be unrelenting disasters and havoc due to the wrongdoing of all sentient beings and lives will be lost. At that moment, for the sake of the kings, their subjects and their land, you should uphold this sutra to bring peace and security to the people. You, not the monks or nuns, nor the male and female lay Buddhist followers, are entrusted with this important and difficult task. They can help to establish the correct teachings of the Buddha but they do not have a king's political power to protect the Triple Gem."

King Prasenajit stood up and said, "Lord Buddha, once the Dharma has degenerated, even though the kings have the power and wealth to protect the Triple Gem, can they actually uphold the Right Dharma?"

"Your worries are well placed, and it is because of this concern that I am earnestly warning you that when the Dharma has degenerated, kings and their courts will begin to behave arrogantly. They will sabotage my teachings with contempt and limit the activities of my followers. They will stop praising the monks and will disrupt the construction of monasteries and Buddha statues. There will be too few kings to uphold the Dharma. That is why you should expand your efforts to protect the monks and nuns, build temples and stupas, construct statues, and make sutra carvings."

Eventually, all sixteen kings became the most ardent and powerful protectors of the Dharma.

From the Buddha's earnest instructions, one can understand the relationship between the Dharma and governmental leaders. Teaching the Dharma requires the support and protection of the government.

Fighting For the Truth

There once was a general who was a Jaina, though he often heard people praising the Buddha for his dignity and virtue. He soon developed a desire to meet the Buddha.

One day, the general met the Buddha and said to him, "I am a soldier. I carry out orders to safeguard our country's frontiers. I heard that your teaching advocates kindness for all who suffer without discrimination. Do you approve the punishment of criminals? Is it ever justifiable to go to war to protect our country? According to your teachings on selfless love, should I tolerate the imprisonment of wicked men?"

The Buddha said, "Though I teach my followers to practice non-violence towards all sentient beings, criminals should be punished and good citizens should be praised. These two positions are not in conflict with one another. Punishment is for one's criminal acts and judgment is the result of one's crime.

While it is wrong to hold a grudge, one must pay for one's crimes. Thus, when a person recognizes and accepts the consequences of his own acts, he will be purified."

The Buddha continued, "I tell people that it is tragic to harm one's own people in a war, but fighting for a just cause and for peace should never be reprimanded. If one goes to war for one's own benefit, he may win and gain wealth and fame, but eventually he will not be rewarded kindly. However, if one loses in a fight for a true and just cause, the failure will never dampen his honor; instead he will have accumulated immeasurable merit."

"Being a successful general is admirable, but conquering one's self is even more admirable. If you can conquer yourself and your enemies with kindness and compassion, this kind of victory will be everlasting and will be the foundation for perpetual peace. Be a fighter for truth and be strong and brave on the battlefield, and the Buddha will always be with you and protect you."

After the Buddha spoke, the general's uncertainty disappeared and he was very happy. He praised the Buddha, "Lord Buddha, you are our helmsman guiding us to the true way to liberation. By following your directions, one will never lose one's guiding light and will find peace and happiness. Lord Buddha, please kindly accept my highest praise."

The news of the general's newfound dedication to Buddhism spread throughout the city of Vaisali.

The Buddha is strongly against aggression. To kill one person, however, for the sake of saving one hundred, and to oppose invasion for a good cause, is sanctioned by the Buddha. From the conversation between the Buddha and the general, one can clearly see the Buddha's wise and intelligent stance on war.

Seven Ways of Governing a Country

While the Buddha and his disciples were once residing at Vulture Peak, King Ajatasatru of Magadha was planning to invade the kingdom of Vrji.

The king thought to himself, "It does not matter how strong this kingdom is and how brave their army is. It should not be difficult to destroy it."

He was so confident that he sent one of his officers to pay homage to the Buddha at Vulture Peak, and asked his officer to seek the Buddha's advice about his intention to invade his neighbor. "The people of Vrji are arrogant and boast of their strength, and have been very disobedient to me," Ajatasatru explained to his officer, "I wish to conquer their country. What does the Buddha say to this?"

Ajatasatru's officer was instructed to listen very closely for any advice that the Buddha might give so that he could report it back to the king immediately since the Buddha always spoke the truth. The officer eventually arrived at Vulture Peak with the king's orders to pay homage to the Buddha. He did as he was instructed and sought advice from the Buddha on behalf of his king.

The Buddha already knew the officer's intention. Thus, he asked Ananda to elaborate on the seven ways in which the kingdom of Vrji was strong and wealthy. The Buddha said, "Ananda, have you ever heard of the people of Vrji gathering to discuss important matters of state?"

Ananda replied, "Yes, I have heard of such events."

"Ananda, when such is the case a country will continue to grow stronger, wealthier, and more stable. No one can invade such a country. Ananda, have you heard of the mutual respect and the harmony between the king and ministers of Vrji?"

"Yes, I have heard of this mutual respect."

"Ananda, when such is the case a country will continue to grow stronger, wealthier and more stable. No one can invade such a country. Ananda, have you heard that the people of Vrji are law abiding and well-mannered citizens?"

"Yes, I have."

"Ananda, when such is the case a country will continue to grow stronger, wealthier and more stable. No one can invade such a country. Ananda, have you heard that the people of Vrji respect their parents, their elders, and teachers?"

"Yes, I have."

"Ananda, when such is the case a country will continue to grow stronger, wealthier and more stable. No one can invade such a country. Ananda, have you heard that the people of Vrji pay respect to their ancestors, ghost and spirits?"

"Yes, I have."

"Ananda, when such is the case a country will continue to grow stronger, wealthier and more stable. No one can invade such a country. Ananda, have you heard that in Vrji, husbands and wives respect each other, and they never engage in indecent conversations?"

"Yes, I have."

"Ananda, when such is the case a country will continue to grow stronger, wealthier and more stable. No one can invade such a country. Ananda, have you heard that the people of Vrji show their respect for the monastics and protect the Dharma?"

"Yes, I definitely have heard such."

"Ananda, when such is the case a country will continue to grow stronger, wealthier and more stable. No one can invade such a country."

After listening to the conversation between the Buddha and Ananda, the officer said to the Buddha, "According to the Buddha's seven ways of making a nation strong and wealthy, just one is enough for Vrji to protect itself from invaders, let alone all seven. I am very busy with affairs of state. I must take my leave."

The Buddha replied, "Of course, but you should be mindful of what has been said regarding the running of a state.

The Buddha's wisdom helped to avert bloodshed.

Those Who Possess Wealth

One day, the Buddha and his followers were on their way to Sravasti to teach the Dharma and accepted offerings when they came across a certain merchant.

This merchant was a dedicated follower of the Buddha and generously donated his time and money to build roads and bridges, establish monasteries, care for orphans, and help the poor. He had long been an admirer of the Buddha's virtues. Now that he was able to see the Buddha's glory and virtue for himself, he was exhilarated and offered the Buddha all the jewels and treasure he had with him. The Buddha compassionately accepted his offering and taught him the Dharma.

The Buddha said, "People deal with their worldly possessions in two ways. Some save every speck of wealth they have. Not only are they frugal with their hard-earned money and spend very little on themselves, but they are also miserly towards their parents, spouse, children, servants and all those who are close to them. However, even after many years, their wealth does not increase despite their frugality. Instead, it decreases. What is the reason for this?

"Wealth is simply material property, and is jointly possessed by five different parties. These five parties hold your wealth and can destroy it at any time. Wealth can be destroyed by fire, swept away by floods, be seized by the government, be robbed by thieves, and be squandered by wayward children.

"Thus, for this first kind of person, even though they have been calculating and accumulated plenty of money, they will not be able to bring even a speck of their wealth upon their death.

"The other type of person handles their wealth much more wisely. They enjoy giving away their hard-earned money. Not only are they generous to their parents, spouse, children, servants and all those who are close to them, they also give as much as possible to help the needy. At the same time, they respect and make offerings to the Triple Gem, and diligently cultivate merits to be liberated from this world. This type of person, due to the merit from their generosity, will be reborn in heaven after their death and enjoy much happiness.

"Regarding worldly property, you should be generous in giving. You should know that in order to receive, you must give first. Therefore you should learn to enjoy giving, and cultivate merit for liberation from the world."

Upon hearing the Buddha's teaching, both the merchant and the Buddha's disciples were filled with joy.

Keep Your Feet on the Ground

While collecting alms the Venerable Maudgalyayana met a strong young man who said to him, "I can break swords and knives into pieces with my bare hands."

Maudgalyayana said to him with a hint of disbelief, "Will you not cut your hands and bleed?"

The young man confidently took up a knife and gave it a squeeze. His expression suddenly changed dramatically. When he released the unbroken knife, it was covered with blood.

Right from the start, Maudgalyayana could tell that the young man was bluffing. When bandaging the young man's hands, Maudgalyayana said to him, "The truth will always come out sooner or later, just as an arrogant and uncompassionate person will lose all his friends."

While the two of them were conversing, the Buddha saw them, and surprisingly asked, "Did you have a fight?"

The young man blushed and remained silent, while Maudgalyayana asked the Buddha respectfully, "Lord Buddha, what happens when foolish people engage in foolish activities?"

The Buddha gave them a glance, and said, "Take the example of a merchant managing his shop. If he knows his role and makes money within reason, he will live in peace and happiness. On the contrary, if he relentlessly seeks fame and fortune to satisfy his selfish needs, he will eventually be consumed by his insatiable desire. He will lose his sanity and be left with nothing at all."

When the young man heard this, he was filled with shame and remorse and said, "Lord Buddha, my original intention was to get Maudgalyayana to praise my capability. I never thought it would end up the reverse."

Examining his wound, the Buddha said with sympathy, "One should always have his feet on the ground. If one works honestly and diligently, the sweet taste of success will follow after all the hard times are gone."

Crows Fighting Over Rotten Meat

During the Buddha's forty-nine year teaching career he taught the Dharma in over three hundred assemblies. He traveled with his disciples to and from many different countries, surviving on alms along the way.

One day, the Buddha was out collecting alms with Ananda, when they saw a few crows fighting over a piece of rotten meat.

One of the crows shouted angrily, "I found this only after much difficulty, why are you trying to snatch it from me?"

"This meat is for all to share. Why do you want to enjoy it all by yourself?" another crow retorted fiercely. As neither would yield, they all ended up in a fight.

Ananda said with a sigh, "How pitiful! For a mere piece of rotten meat they are ready to fight to the death. I guess this fight will only end when they have all dropped dead."

On hearing this, the Buddha said to Ananda, "The riches of this world are but a piece of rotten meat in the eyes of the sages, yet so many people fight for it adamantly. During the Period of Declining Dharma, sentient beings will pay little attention to the practice of the noble Way. They will fight to compete for power, fame and wealth. They are just as foolish and laughable as the crows fighting over the piece of rotten meat."

In the eyes of the Buddha, worldly fame and fortune are like a piece of rotten meat, unworthy of pursuit. The ideal of the Buddha is to guide all beings in search of a Pure Land, where there is no sign of aging, no pain from illness, and no fear of death. Things neither increase nor decrease. It is an immaculate world that is neither pleasant nor unpleasant. It is a state of permanance, bliss, and purity and is the true self. It is the true perfect world and we should strive for it. However, sentient beings mistake illusions for the truth and confuse right with wrong. They do not realize the significance of life and death nor the immediacy of impermanence. They cannot perceive the value of truth and only engage in the daily pursuit of the illusory fame and fortune by deceit and rivalry. From the Buddha's point of view, they are exactly like the foolish crows fighting over a piece of rotten meat.

The Stinky Woman has a Clean Mind

There was once a low caste woman in Sravasti whose job was to clean the streets and gutters each morning. She looked very dirty, but she had no time to care for her appearance. The people of the city would avoid her. They forgot all about the merit she gained from serving them, and instead would mock her and call her "stinky woman," even covering their noses and spitting on her when she passed by.

The Buddha sympathized with this woman and invited her to hear his teachings. When the townspeople heard of this and many of them came to see. As they passed by the river, they saw a beautiful maiden washing her clothes. Once they arrived where the Buddha was residing they arrogantly said, "Lord

Buddha, we often hear your teachings on cleanliness and purity. Why do you now wish to talk with the most disgusting and smelly woman in the city? Don't you think this will ruin your reputation?"

The Buddha calmly replied with a question, "Did any of you see a woman washing clothes in the river on your way here?"

"Yes," one of the townspeople answered, "We all saw that lovely woman. She seemed to have a divine light within her."

"That lovely woman is the one who you called 'stinky woman,' the one who cleans the city for all of you. She gives you all cleanliness, but you reject her for her appearance. True purity is not found in one's appearance, but in the mind. Though she cleans the dirt of the city daily, her mind has been purified long ago. You dislike her dirty appearance, yet your minds are impure. How does your noble appearance help you?"

"To have a pure mind is to be truly clean. Maintaining an elegant appearance while the mind remains impure is not worthy of respect."

One who has a pure mind has a pure spirit. One can be called truly pure when the mind is pure. One with a defiled and impure mind but a splendid, noble appearance is not worthy of respect.

Part Nine:

Practice

When we follow the Buddha's teachings it is said that we practice. It is called practice because the path to awakening is a series of steps, and we become wiser and more compassionate along the way. The Buddha taught us not to focus on the road ahead, but on each individual step: the ways in which our actions, words, and thoughts can make our make our lives and the lives of others better.

These stories show the Buddha urging his disciples to practice, to focus on each step to ensure that it brings us one step closer to awakening.

The Buddha Shares His Seat with Mahakasyapa

The Venerable Mahakasyapa was a monk of long standing and great attainment who, even though he was growing old, maintained his ascetic practices. The Buddha saw how Mahakasyapa continued to live with such hardship in his old age, and decided to advise him to be easier on himself.

While the Buddha was residing at Deer Park, he summoned Mahakasyapa. As Mahakasyapa slowly walked forward with long hair and ragged clothes, the newly ordained monks did not recognize him as the great Mahakasyapa and gave him despicable looks. Some even tried to stop him from approaching the Buddha.

The Buddha knew what the monks were thinking. He got up and went to greet the old ascetic, "Mahakasyapa, I have saved a seat for you. Come and sit with me." When the monks heard the Buddha, they were stunned that this old monk was actually the famous Mahakasyapa. He walked toward the Buddha and bowed before him. He then stepped back and said, "Lord Buddha, I am only your disciple. It is inappropriate for me to share your seat."

At that moment, the Buddha described to everyone Mahakasyapa's tremendous virtue, attainment, and practice that equaled his own. Even if he had not met the Buddha, he still could have attained awakening on his own, as an arhat.

When this was said, everyone realized how important Mahakasyapa was in the Buddha's eyes. Simply by looking at how the Buddha treated Mahakasyapa as an honorable guest indicated the importance of his status in the sangha.

The Buddha told him to discontinue his ascetic practices, change his ragged robes for new ones offered by devotees, and to rest in his old age without exhausting himself.

Even with such a show of concern from the Buddha, Mahakasyapa was still reluctant to change his ascetic practice. He said to the Buddha, "I do not suffer from my ascetic practices. On the contrary, I enjoy them greatly and am very happy. I do not have to worry about a shortage of clothes or food. I have no gains or losses. I simply abide in tranquility and peace. Some might criticize this kind of life as being selfish. I am unlike Sariputra, Maudgalyayana, Purna, and Katyayana, who are very devoted to spreading the Buddha's teaching. They are fearless and often will risk their own lives to teach the Dharma for the benefit of others. Although, I don't have that kind of devotion, I have never forgotten the benevolence shown to me by the Buddha. In order to repay the Buddha's kindness, I have taken up these ascetic practices.

"All sentient beings depend on the teachings of the sangha to be liberated. To be a teacher in the sangha one must be an ardent practitioner and carry the responsibility of spreading the Dharma. How can the sangha be purified? Through disciplined daily life and developing one's own virtue. Ascetic practice is the most disciplined way of life. If one can get used to living an ascetic life, one can endure, tolerate, and be content with a simple life and be mindful of both the Dharma and others' well being. Lord Buddha, I only want to strengthen the sangha so that it can benefit all sentient beings. I gladly accept the difficulties of my ascetic practices and beg the Buddha to forgive my stubbornness.

The Buddha was very pleased. He looked at Mahakasyapa and the other monks and said, "Good. Have you monks heard the elder's words? The destruction of the Dharma will not occur at the hands of demons, but in the corruption and the destruction of the sangha itself. Mahakasyapa is correct. In order to spread the Dharma and let the light of truth continue to shine in this world, the sangha must be strong. For the sangha to be strong, you must live a disciplined life. If everyone could be like Mahakasyapa, then my Dharma will continue to flourish. Mahakasyapa, continue your practice in your own way. Come to see me often."

The Buddha and Mahakasyapa are two different individuals, but their thoughts are one. The Buddha treated Mahakasyapa like a guest and a friend, yet Mahakasyapa never forgot to respect the Buddha as his teacher. The warm friendship shared between a teacher and a disciple constantly permeated all they did.

When we talk about the Buddha or arhats, many people picture them as being as cold as stone, but this is not the case. Buddhas and arhats have ultimately filtered out their defilements so that only love and the noble parts of humanity remain. This type of love is called loving-kindness and compassion. Compassion is rooted in wisdom, and acts as a magnet that attracts all sentient beings. It enables all beings to be in touch with their more noble qualities, and be able to change their own bad habits.

The Most Important Part of Learning

A certain monk had been a disciple of the Buddha for many years, but he was a very slow learner. The Buddha once assigned five hundred arhats to tutor him daily. But, after three years, he still could not remember even a single verse. The Buddha sympathized with him, and personally taught him this verse:

Restrain your tongue, and regulate your mind.
Restrain your body from committing evil deeds.
If you can observe and follow thus,
The time of your liberation will have arrived.

The monk responded to the Buddha's act of kindness with heartfelt gratitude. In his great joy he instantly memorized the verse and could recite it easily.

The Buddha said to him, "At last, in your old age you have memorized one verse. For others this task was too easy. You must not stop at this stage. Now I am going to explain the meaning of this verse. You must listen carefully."

With undivided attention the monk listened to the Buddha, who taught him the ten unwholesome actions: killing, stealing, sexual misconduct, lying, duplicitous speech, harsh speech, flattery, greed, anger, and delusion. He asked the monk to reflect on how the ten unwholesome actions arise, and how to eliminate them.

The Buddha continued, "Sentient beings continue to come and go in the three worlds and six realms like the incessant turning of a wheel. Those who have restrained from the ten unwholesome actions are reborn in heaven, while those who have committed them are reborn in hell. Transforming the ten unwholesome actions into the ten wholesome actions is fulfill the goal of my teachings."

With patience and kindness, the Buddha explained to him the wholesome and unwholesome actions that come from the body, speech, and the mind, and the other countless wonderful meanings of the Dharma. The monk suddenly awakened and became an arhat..

Everyone in the sangha knew that this monk was a slow learner, so they wondered how he could have awakened with only a single verse. Greatly surprised, everyone went to see the Buddha for an explanation.

The Buddha said to them, "In spiritual cultivation, the quality of your practice is much more important that the quantity of your knowledge. Although this monk could only remember one verse, he revealed the hidden treasure of the Dharma. With a focused mind, he has purified his actions, speech, and thoughts such that they are as pure as heavenly gold. Ordinary people learn extensively but their understanding is shallow. Some even recite the words without practicing it. Doing this only leads to confusion and is spiritually futile."

The Buddha then recited another verse to the gathering:

> *Chanting one thousand chapters*
> *Without understanding their meaning,*
> *Is not as good as the correct understanding of a single*
> *verse,*
> *Through which one's unwholesome actions will be erased.*

> *Chanting one thousand lines*
> *Without realizing their meaning– what is the benefit?*
> *It is not as good as learning one principle*
> *Practicing it, and being liberated.*

> *Chanting many sutras*
> *Without understanding– what good will it bring?*
> *Understanding a single sentence of the Dharma and*
> *Cultivating accordingly will enable one to realize the Way.*

Sutra-chanting is certainly meritorious. This merit will multiply if one actually learns the teachings, understands their meaning, and practices them in one's daily life.

Cultivate as if Playing The Harp

Among the Buddha's disciples, there was a monk named Sronakotivimsa. Formerly he was a famous musician who was born into a wealthy family. His parents cherished him like a precious treasure. One day he was deeply touched by the Buddha's teachings and decided to become a monk. As a monk, he would only eat one meal a day, and cultivate in the open air while sitting under a tree. Both his parents strongly opposed his decision, but they were unable to undermine Sronakotivimsa's determination to cultivate.

Sronakotivimsa had grown accustomed to a comfortable lifestyle all his life. His body grew weak from his rigorous cultivation, yet he was still no closer to awakening. It soon became difficult for him to sustain himself physically, and he became very frustrated. He thought of returning to household life and becoming a lay follower instead. He hoped to attain awakening through the practice of generosity.

The Buddha knew of Sronakotivimsa's vexation. In order to console and encourage him, the Buddha visited Sronakotivimsa and said to him, "You spend your days alone, absorbed in ardent cultivation and seem to be interested in little other than sitting meditation. Let me ask you, when you play the harp, what will happen if the string is too tight?"

"Lord Buddha, The string will break if it is too tight," Sronakotivimsa replied.

"What if the string is too lax?"

"Then there would be no sound."

The Buddha spoke compassionately, "Cultivation is just like playing the harp: it should not be too intense nor too relaxed. When it is too intense or too relaxed, problems will arise. Moderate your mind, and seek the Middle Way in everything you do. As a monk, use your music to help me propagate the Dharma and strengthen your own faith and that of others. This is indeed very good."

Sronakotivimsa thus cultivated according to the Buddha's advice. He was then able to calm his mind and was soon awakened.

We must seek the wisdom of the Middle Way in our lives. Indulging in pleasures can cause one to be drowned in the enjoyment of the five sensual desires, while extreme asceticism can cause perplexity and fear. Between the extremes of indulging in pleasures and asceticism lies the Middle Way. Just like when playing the harp; if the strings are not too tight nor too lax, there will be beautiful music.

The Simile of the Drum

There once was a wealthy elder from Rajagrha who had a drum of the highest quality. When played, the drum made wonderful music. Every time the elder held a banquet, the sound of the drum was so clear and pleasant that it could move the guests to sing and dance. This made the banquets very enjoyable for both the elder and his guests.

As time passed, the drum became very worn out until it

could no longer make its beautiful music. This saddened the
elder beyond words.

When the Buddha heard about this drum he told his monks,
"Those monks who apply themselves to cultivating a virtuous
body and mind and upholding the precepts are like the beautiful
sound of the drum."

"Lord Buddha, what do you mean?" Rahula asked
bewildered.

Without a word, the Buddha clapped his hands and asked
Rahula, "Can you hear that sound?"

"Yes, Lord Buddha."

The Buddha continued, "A monk can become weakened with
old age, but if he has pure conduct his moral example will be
fondly remembered forever like the sound of applause.
Furthermore, he will become a role model for future generations."

Rahula responded tentatively, "Lord Buddha, do you mean
that the feebleness brought on by old age is like the drum skin
that is worn out with time, but a monk's pure conduct is like the
sound of the drum, forever vividly remembered as if the
beautiful melody has a life of its own?"

The Buddha listened to Rahula's interpretation, and nodded
his head in approval.

*Our body is like the skin of a drum: according to the law of
impermanence, one day it will disintegrate. Our true nature is
like the pleasant sound of a drum; it enters our ears and dwells
in our heart. It is not easily forgotten. Since we now have a drum
that can play, how can we make wondrous music so that it will
be remembered? This is the task of spiritual practice.*

The Five Ways to Practice

The Venerable Meghiya was the Buddha's attendant when the Buddha arrived in Magadha to teach the Dharma. One morning, Meghiya saw a clear lake beside a beautiful grove with tall trees and a light breeze. He thought this would be a good place to practice. Meghiya joyfully went back to the Buddha and asked if he could meditate there.

The Buddha answered "Meghiya, I do not have another attendant at this time. Be patient and you will be able to go there in a few days when another monk has come to replace you."

Meghiya would not give up, and he continued to ask for permission again and again. He pleaded, "Lord Buddha, I cannot wait any longer. I must go there today."

Despite Meghiya's annoyances, the Buddha patiently advised waiting for a few days, but Meghiya lost his patience and rudely said, "Lord Buddha, you are a saint who no longer needs to practice. But I still need to practice. I am going today to meditate there!"

"If you insist, then go," the Buddha responded.

With the Buddha's consent, Meghiya went joyfully to his grove. Once he sat down his mind fulfilled with thoughts of greed, anger, and ignorance. He then thought of the Buddha's great kindness and compassion. At the end of the day, he packed his possessions, went back the Buddha, and reported his experience.

After listening, the Buddha said, "Meghiya, one must practice in five ways so that one can be free from affliction"

Meghiya respectfully asked, "Lord Buddha, what are those five ways?"

The Buddha answered, "First, one should follow a knowledgeable and kind person and get along well with him.

"Second, one should uphold the precepts. Closely watch your thoughts, act with proper and polite conduct, and avoid even minor misbehavior.

"Third, one should teach the principles of discipline, meditative concentration, wisdom, liberation, decreasing desire, contentment, and cause and effect so that one's mind is free of affliction.

"Fourth, one should diligently practice the wholesome Dharma and refrain from false thinking.

"Fifth, one should cultivate wisdom and observe phenomena arising and ceasing."

Meghiya felt ashamed and vowed to follow the Buddha's teachings.

An ancient proverb says, "A noisy place is a place for Buddhist practice." If one can get rid of one's illusions and gain tranquility, one can practice anywhere. However, if the mind is full of wandering thoughts, one cannot practice even in a quiet mountain or in a remote temple. Therefore, Buddhist practice does not require a quiet mountain or waterside grove.

Judge Not by Appearance

Once, when the Buddha was staying at Jetavana Monastery near Sravasti, an ugly monk named Bhadra came to see him from afar. When the monks around the Buddha saw Bhadra approaching, they instantly despised him and whispered, "Who is this ugly monk? Just looking at him makes me nauseous."

The Buddha knew the monk's thoughts and said to them, "Do you see that ugly monk for whom you have negative feelings?"

The monks answered, "Yes, we see him."

The Buddha said, "Monks, you should not think poorly of that monk. That monk has freed himself of all burdens and worries, and is an arhat. If you are as knowledgeable as a Buddha, you may assess others. Otherwise, criticizing someone unreasonably only hurts yourself."

The Buddha gave an analogy, "Although peacocks adorn their bodies with colorful feathers, they cannot match wild swans in their ability to fly. A person with a beautiful face and elegant features cannot compare to one who is free of worries and afflictions.

"That monk is like a fine horse. He knows how to behave and control his thoughts. He is immune to desire and temptation and free from the cycle of birth and death. He is in his last physical body and has tamed the multitude of unwholesome mental afflictions."

After having heard the Buddha's words, none of his disciples dared to judge people by their looks again.

It is wrong to judge others by their appearance. People who cultivate and purify themselves will attain a dignified physical appearance through correct practice. For those who have cultivated themselves, ugliness and beauty are no longer important.

The Swiftness of Impermanence

Once, while the Buddha was teaching the Dharma, he posed the following to his disciples, "Suppose a person were to say to four skilled archers, 'If you each were to simultaneously shoot an arrow, facing east, south, west and north, I could catch them all before they fell to the ground.' I do not believe there is anyone like that, but if such a person was really capable of this, he must be an extremely fast man with quick reaction time. Do you agree?"

"Yes, Lord Buddha, that man must have incredible speed. He would need to be fast to catch just one arrow shot in any single direction, let alone catch all the arrows in four directions at once. He must be the fastest man in the world."

"You are correct. Is there anything else in this world that is faster than this arrow catcher?"

All of the disciples were perplexed and listened with undivided attention. The Buddha continued, "The sun and the moon move far faster than the arrow catcher, and the rapidness with which human life changes far exceeds that of the sun and the moon's movement."

Upon hearing the comparison, the disciples finally understood. One of them quickly put up his hand and said, "Lord Buddha, through the story of the arrow, you are telling us the impermanence is ever present, and that the things of this world pass very quickly. We must diligently cultivate without relaxing our efforts. We have learned much from your teachings, about the incredible swiftness of impermanence, and we will observe and conduct ourselves strictly in accordance with your teachings."

The Buddha said that life exists between each breath and change occurs with unexpected rapidness. Life comes and goes in the blink of an eye. Appreciation of the impermanence of life will improve our understanding of the value of life and prompt us to accomplish our goals.

The Rainstorm of Birth and Death

Every year the rainy season arrives in the Indian sub-continent without fail. One year, heavy rain fell non-stop, day and night, for a very long time. There were disastrous floods everywhere. The Buddha and his disciples practiced diligently during their rains retreat. Watching the downpour outside, the disciples were worried and expressed their concerns for the lives and property of the ordinary people.

Upali remarked, "It is the rainy season now, and clear days are nowhere in sight. Countless lives will be lost in this disaster."

Purna walked to the door and saw the rain come down in buckets, "Since the beginning of existence, sentient beings have been revolving in the cycles of birth and death within the six realms. It is like being in the midst of a wild horse stampede; it is beyond human control."

Sariputra also expressed his opinion, "Wherever there is heavy rainfall, roads are washed away. The floods make traveling impossible and human misery is everywhere."

The Buddha saw that his disciples were involved in a deep discussion, so he took the opportunity to address them, "Since the unfathomable beginning of the cycle of birth and death, sentient beings have turned on the wheel of rebirth and are ignorant of the origin of suffering. For example, during a flood, countless lives and property are lost and destroyed. The disaster is mainly caused by the lack of prevention and preparation. People do no learn from their past painful experiences and fail to change. Instead they leave it all to chance and natural disasters keep recurring. In this way sentient beings keep turning on the wheel of rebirth. Therefore, monks, you must eliminate all that is unwholesome, and you should never hesitate to do what is wholesome."

The Buddha then spoke the following verse:

> *A bowyer adjusts the angles of a bow,*
> *A sailor masters the art of sailing,*
> *A carpenter is familiar with the structure of the wood,*
> *A wise man cultivates himself.*

After listening to the Buddha's words, his disciples concentrated on practicing right mindfulness and hoped to use their wisdom to cross the river of birth and death.

The Four Most Terrifying Things

One day, when the Buddha was teaching the Dharma at Jetavana Monastery, King Prasenajit came to visit him. The Buddha saw that the king was wearing a mourning garment, and he wore grief and sorrow on his face. Several days ago, the king's ninety-year old mother had become gravely ill and passed away.

The king and his senior ministers prepared the funeral ceremony and sent the bier to the cemetery. After the funeral, they all went to visit the Buddha.

After listening to the king's story, the Buddha looked upon the king' sad expression and said, "In the life of human beings, there are four things that are terrifying: after birth we will grow old and die, when we are sick the body becomes withered and thin, after we die consciousness leaves the body, and once we are gone we will be separated from our families forever.

"These four things are the most terrifying things that can happen to us. No one can avoid the law of impermanence. Even those who are closest to us can not live with us forever. Life is like flowing water: once it passes it will never return to the way it was. Since no one can avoid death, feeling sorrow for the deceased is not going to help anyone. We might as well do good deeds and accumulate merit for them. Dedicating merit for the deceased person is like preparing food for a person who is going on a long journey; it is truly helpful to him or her."

After the Buddha spoke, the king finally felt relieved and a smile appeared on his face.

Where there is birth, death is inevitable; where something arises, cessation is bound to follow. Life is a cycle. While living is not necessarily pleasant, dying is not really sorrowful. Birth is not the beginning, nor is death the end. Birth brings death and death brings rebirth, all in a continuous cycle. If we can learn from this continuous cycle of arising and cessation to prove the indestructibility of life, then we will have acquired a new level of wisdom.

The Brevity of Human Life

Once, while the Buddha was residing at Sravasti, some monks gathered to discuss among themselves how brief a human life was. They held that life was short for both humans and celestial beings, and that all life was inevitably followed by death.

The Buddha heard the monks discussion from afar and joined them to ask, "Monks, what is it that you were just discussing?"

One of the disciples replied, "We had just eaten our meal and were discussing the brevity of human life, impermanence, and transience."

The Buddha sighed, "Yes, life is short and is over in the blink of an eye. We should all concentrate on our practice, and be mindful of performing good deeds. All monastics should remember two things upon awakening each morning: the first is to teach the Dharma and the second is to meditate. Do you wish to listen to the Dharma?"

"Yes, Lord Buddha! We would be very pleased to listen to your teaching."

The Buddha said, "Long ago there was a kingdom that had a huge and magnificent tree. The tree trunk measured over 560 miles around, with roots that reached down 840 miles. It reached over 4,000 miles into the sky and had branches that were over 2,000 miles long. People in this kingdom lived for 84,000 years, and women would marry and leave their homes when they were 500 years old. However, they still suffered from cold, heat, hunger, thirst, lust, gluttony, old age and sickness.

"At that time there was an elder who was tremendously

wealthly. He thought, 'human life is short, and birth is followed by death. Wealth is impermanent, it is better to give one's property away to the poor and needy. Worldly happiness is short-lived, it is better to leave the home life and be rid of defilement.' So he left home to learn from wise teachers and to become a monk, strictly upholding the precepts. All who listened to him teach the Dharma grew to understand impermanence and revere the noble path, and thus would ordain and follow his teachings.

"He would tell his disciples, 'Life is short, fleeting, and impermanent. Death inevitably follows birth; life is not everlasting. Therefore we should rid ourselves of greed, donate to the poor, control our desires, and not perform unwholesome deeds. Life is transient like the morning dew. It is like rain falling into the great sea: the foam on the surface of the water disappers instantly. Life is like a flash of lightning or a spark: in an instant it is gone. One's life diminishes each day and night, while it fills up with worries and suffering. How can it be long lasting? Life is like a cow on the way to the slaughterhouse, step by step heading for death. It is like water rushing down from the mountains, speeding forth day and night without stopping. Thus we should all practice the right path to achieve peace and happiness in a future life.'"

The Buddha continued, "Such a long life span of 84,000 years was considered impermanent and brief by that elder. What about now, when humans are not expected to live beyond a hundred years? Even if one lives to be one hundred years old, if one eats two meals a day, then one would need to have approximately 73,000 meals in one hundred years years. Fifrty of those years are spent sleeping or in the dark of night. Ten of those years are spent during childhood or during sickness. Working and worrying about family matters takes up another twenty years.

With all of that time removed, only ten years remain. Is human life not very short?"

After hearing the insightful teaching of the Buddha, the monks were all very overjoyed. They bowed before the Buddha and departed.

Born from Brahma

Among the Buddha's followers, many had previously been practitioners from other wandering sects but gradually became disciples of the Buddha. Vasistha and Bharadvaja were two such examples. These two young Brahmans were often scorned when they first left their homes to follow the Buddha. They were often chastised thus, "The Brahman caste is the most superior caste. We are born from the mouth of Brahma, the creator of this universe. We are the successors of Brahma. Now, you have degraded yourselves by associating with those of the lower castes to the extent of allowing yourselves to learn from them!"

When the Buddha heard this, he told his followers, "If those of the Brahman caste are born from the mouth of Brahma, then do Brahman women give birth by way of their wombs? There are good and bad people in every caste. One can be called superior only if that person purifies his thoughts, speech, and actions until all attachments are discarded and true wisdom is developed. Only then can a person truly benefit himself and others."

This doctrine of the equality of all beings was welcomed and echoed by the people of all classes, many of whom joined the sangha to help put an end to the discriminatory caste system. The Buddha was a true social reformer.

The Right Path for Mahallakas

There once was a monastery with five hundred monks about six or seven miles outside of the city in the country of Mala. One such monk was an older monk named Mahallakas. He was a very slow person, and no matter how many times he was taught, he could not remember even a single line from the sutras. All five hundred monks looked down on him and gave him no respect. No one wanted to be around him, so he was always alone.

One day, the king sent one of his ministers to the monastery to invite all the monks for a meal, but the dim-witted Mahallakas, ashamed of his own ignorance, was too afraid to go to the banquet. Once the other monks had left for the palace, he remembered his own shameful ignorance again. Saddened, he walked to the garden with some rope and planned to hang himself from a tree.

Just as he was about to hang himself, the awe-inspiring Buddha appeared before him and admonished him, "Mahallakas, how could you do such a foolish thing? Why don't you learn to improve yourself instead? You were a very knowledgeable, wise, and well-cultivated person in a previous life but, because you were arrogant, did not wish to teach others, looked down on everybody, and cultivated a mind of arrogance, you became ignorant and foolish in every lifetime since, including this very life. You should repent your previous behavior and reform. Trying to kill yourself does not resolve your bad karma."

After the Buddha told Mahallakas this, he felt very ashamed, then bowed down in front of the Buddha and asked the Buddha to give him a chance for forgiveness. The ever compassionate

Buddha did not mind his past poor behavior. As long as he was willing to correct himself, the Buddha was willing to accept him. Thus, seeing an opportunity, the Buddha very patiently taught Mahallakas the Dharma. Since he had the proper karmic conditions, as the Buddha taught him, Mahallakas' dark and ignorant heart became clear. Mahallakas realized the true nature of the phenomena of the world and became an arhat. The Buddha realized that Mahallakas was now awakened and told him to hurry to the palace to receive offerings and teach the Dharma to others.

Mahallakas arrived at the king's palace just as the banquet was about to begin. Though he was not invited, he sat in one of the high seats, reserved for the most honored and respected people. When everyone saw what he was doing, they were aghast. The other monks thought that he must be mad, but no one wanted to say anything in front of the king and his ministers.

As the dinner went on, everyone continued to enjoy themselves. After dinner, Mahallakas stood up in front of the assembly without any sign of fear. He then spoke with the force of a lion's roar and began to teach the wonderful Dharma. All the people sat and listened and showed great respect, especially the monks. They felt really ashamed that they did not know or perceive that he had become an arhat. They all felt regret that they had underestimated him in the past.

Part Ten:

Repentance

The Buddhist path can seem long, and we may falter along the way. But we should not feel despair – the Buddha would not give up on any sentient being, how can we give up on ourselves? If we stumble along the way, we should pick ourselves up, acknowledge our mistakes, and resolve to do better in the future. These stories of sincere repentance teach us that, no matter what we have done in the past, we all have the potential to awaken to the truth.

Sariputra's Repentance

One day, the Buddha gave Sariputra permission to go away to teach the Dharma. After Sariputra had left, a monk came to the Buddha to slander Sariputra.

He told the Buddha, "Sariputra had a dispute with a group of monks and did not repent! Now he is away teaching the Dharma."

As soon as the Buddha heard this, he sent for Sariputra and gathered the entire assembly together. When Sariputra returned to the monastery, the Buddha spoke to him, "Shortly after you left, a monk came to me and said that you had a dispute with a group of monks and did not repent. Instead you went away to teach the Dharma. Is this true?"

"Lord Buddha, I think you know me best," replied Sariputra.

"I do understand but there is still doubt in everyone else's minds, so will you please, in front of everyone, explain yourself."

"From the time that I was born until now, it has been almost eighty years. I often reflect on the fact that in my entire life, I have not killed, lied, or even told a single small lie. Furthermore, I have never had a dispute with anyone. Lord Buddha, since I am a pure and cultivated individual, why would I argue?"

Sariputra continued, "I am like the earth. Both pure things and impure things fall on the earth, and the earth does not discriminate. I am also like water. Water cleans both the wholesome and the unwholesome and does not discriminate. I am like a glowing fire. Fire burns everything on the mountains; it burns both beautiful things and ugly things without discrimination. I am also like a broom; a broom sweeps away everything regardless of its appearance. My mind has been well cultivated to tolerate all without differentiation or discrimination. Why would I argue with the other monks and then run off? Lord Buddha, you know me, and deep down, the monk who told you this also knows me. If I really did what the monk claims, then may he accept my repentance."

The Buddha then said to that monk, "You should repent."

That monk rose, bowed before the Buddha, and said, "I now apologize for accusing Sariputra. May the Buddha please accept my repentance."

The Buddha told the monk to personally repent to Sariputra, not him. So the monk did as he was told. The Buddha then spoke to Sariputra, "You may now accept the monk's repentance, and help him purify his mind."

In the end, the dispute was settled by the Buddha's compassion and wisdom and all were at peace again.

Celestial Eyes from Repentance

The Venerable Aniruddha once fell asleep while the Buddha was teaching. After being disciplined by the Buddha, he swore to never sleep again. His eyes grew weak and he eventually lost his eyesight. Instead of feeling sorry for himself, he dedicated himself to cultivation and ultimately opened the celestial eye. With the celestial eye, he could see all sentient beings in all six realms of existence.

One morning, when the Buddha was residing at the Jetavana Monastery, Ananda inquired, "Lord Buddha, what is the difference between what you see and what Aniruddha sees with his celestial eye?"

The Buddha replied, "The world as seen by a Buddha is

beyond the comprehension of an unawakened monk or even that of an arhat or pratyekabuddha. The Buddha can clearly see all sentient beings in the world, even the tiniest creatures in the darkest areas. What Aniruddha sees is only a small portion. How can that compare with what a Buddha sees?"

Ananda asked, "What has Aniruddha done in the past to receive the supernatural power of the celestial eye?"

The Buddha then slowly recounted the story of Aniruddha:

"One night, a long time ago, after Vipasyin Buddha had entered parinirvana, a thief broke into a monastery to steal its valuables. The main shrine was pitch black except for a fading oil lamp in front of a statue of Vipasyin Buddha. The thief took an arrowhead to adjust the wick and the entire room was illuminated brightly.

"Once the room was lit, the burglar saw the dignified yet kind appearance of Vipasyin Buddha's statue and instantly felt remorse for his bad intentions. He thought, 'So many devotees have offered their wealth to the Buddha for his blessings. How can I steal these offerings? How can I steal any of the goods from the monastery?' After he left the monastery, he reformed his ways and never stole again.

"With that spark of goodness in his mind, for ninety-one kalpas his bad karma decreased gradually while his merit grew. He finally was born as Aniruddha in this time. He renounced the household life to become a monk under me and attained the divine eye. Among the my ten great disciples, he is known as the foremost in celestial vision."

Repentance is very important in our lives. It is like Dharma water that washes away all our bad karma. It is like a ship ready to take us to the shore of nirvana. It is like medicine for curing

our confused minds. It is like a lamp which can brighten our
endless darkness. It is like a brick wall which can protect our six
sense organs. It is like a bridge which guides us to Buddhahood.
It is like clothing which can adorn the fruit of our enlightenment.
A quote from the Vegetable Roots Sayings, a well known Chinese
work discussing life philosophy reads, "Ultimate merit can be
destroyed by pride; the worst mistake can be erased through
repentance." There is no evil too deep to be purified by
repentance.

A theif fixed a lamp before the Buddha statue and was able
to develop the seed of repentance upon seeing the wonderful
appearance of the Buddha. Further, he ended up with great merit
and virtue and cultivation. For those who make offerings of light
in temples all year, the resulting merit will be unimaginable.

The Repentance of a Princess

King Prasenajit had a very ugly daughter. Though she was a
princess, it was impossible for her to find a suitor because of her
appearance. The king had no choice but to seek a young suitor
amongst the poor and promote his status to a prince in order for
the marriage to take place.

After the marriage, the prince would attend all the palace
functions alone as his bride was simply too ugly to be seen in
public. After a while, people began to wonder why he would
never bring her along to any state functions. They wondered if it
was possible that she was so beautiful that her beauty would
inspire jealousy in people, so the prince decided to keep her all
to himself. Several courtiers who were close to the prince
decided to find out for themselves. They made him drunk one

night, and stole his key to her chamber.

All the while, the princess who had been forced to stay at home felt very sad for causing her husband's embarrassment. Everyday she repented for the karma she incurred from all her previous lives by bowing to a Buddha statue. Strangely enough, as she sincerely repented, her rough hands gradually became supple and shiny. Her small unattractive eyes also slowly became immensely beautiful. The more she expressed remorse for her previous wrongdoings, the more gracious and elegant her appearance became. When the officers came to peek into her chamber, they saw an extremely beautiful woman bowing before a Buddha statue. They were in awe and dumb-founded by her beauty. When they returned to the court, they whispered to the rest of the officers about how beautiful their princess was and that their prince was very selfish to keep her all to himself.

Words of the beautiful princess reached the king and queen. Queen Mallika was delighted. They knew that the change was made possible because of the Buddha's compassion.

To show their gratitude, the king and queen made a visit to Sravasti with offerings to the Buddha and all the monastics. The king joined his palms and asked the Buddha, "Compassionate Buddha, please tell us what our daughter did in her past lives that caused her to be reborn as a princess, live a life of luxury and yet have such an ugly and rough complexion?"

The Buddha replied, "One's appearance is a direct result of one's past karma. Our wholesome and unwholesome deeds follow us everywhere like our shadows. Our appearance is not a coincidental occurrence."

The Buddha went on to explain that the princess had been scornful to an arhat in a previous life. Later, she regretted her wrongdoing and asked for forgiveness from that arhat. Her previous repentance then gave rise to the favorable conditions for her present transformation.

The Buddha's teaching enhanced the audience's confidence. They had no further doubts about the law of cause and effect, the concept of karma, or the merit that can be gained by making offerings to the Buddha and the sangha, having faith in the teachings, and cultivating.

Human life lasts only a short while, like soft smoke and fleeting fog. Some people go after desire and fame and live a life filled with foolishness and worries. Others refrain from desire and observe the empty nature of all phenomena and lead a life of simplicity and quietude.

Whether one is honorable or lowly depends on whether one relinquishes or clings to the things of the world. Amidst the emotions of our daily life, we should learn to repent and realize, "I have done wrong. It is my fault. This has happened as a result of my carelessness..." When we repent and make amends on a daily basis, we improve our character, increase our tolerance, and the quality of our lives improves substantially. On the other hand, if we allow ourselves to be controlled and shackled by our emotions, we will descend into the hells of the five desires, unable to rise above or break free. This is a fearful, defiled and tragic existence, with suffering beyond description. Repentance not only changes a person's temperament, it can even affect one's appearance.

The Repentance of King Ajatasatru

Ajatasatru was an evil king who murdered his father, King Bimbisara, to ascend to the throne. Sometime after Ajatasatru murdered his father, he dreamed of the dead king. In his dream his father smiled and said to him, "Ajatasatru, I am your father. Even though you murdered me, I do not hate you for what you have done, because I am a disciple of the Buddha. With the Buddha's compassion and kindness, I vow to forgive you. After all, you are my son. I pray for you. May you soon amend your ways, repent, and conduct yourself according to the right path."

King Ajatasatru was saddened. He reflected on his father's love and kindness, and felt great shame for his evil act.

One day when King Ajatasatru was dining with his mother Queen Vaidehi, he noticed that his son Udayibhadda was not present. He asked the servants, "Where is Udayibhadda? Go and bring him here."

A servant replied, "Udayibhadda is playing with the dog."

The servant then went to fetch Udayibhadda who came with a puppy in his arms.

King Ajatasatru asked his son, "Why didn't you come to dinner?"

Udayibhadda said, pouting, "I cannot eat without my dog at the table."

King Ajatasatru let the dog eat with them. After a while, he said to his mother, "I am a king but, for the love of my son, I let the dog have a meal with me at my table. This is embarrassing."

Queen Vaidehi replied, "It is nothing to have a dog at the dinner table. For the love of your son, you feel embarrassed to share the table with a dog. Out of love for you, your father behaved even more humbly. When you were little, you had boils on your fingers, and you could not sleep because of the pain. Your father held you in his lap day and night. To ease your pain, he held your finger in his mouth; he chose to swallow the pus rather than let go of your finger and disturb your sleep. This is how much your father loved you. He did what others would not do."

After listening to his mother, King Ajatasatru silently left the dinner table and went to the next room. From then on he no longer enjoyed the glory of being king. His heart felt weighed down by a great burden.

The effects of King Ajatasatru's bad karma began to befall him. His body became covered with boils and his mind was filled with remorse. He told his ministers, "Now both my mind and body are seriously ill. It must be the effects of my karma from murdering my father. Can any of you treat my illness?"

Among his ministers were six non-Buddhist ascetics who used the ideals of their religions to try to convince the king that he was not guilty of murdering his father, but their persuasion failed to sway the king. Instead they reinforced the king's decision to repent.

The famous physician Jivaka came to see the King, "Your Majesty, how is your health?"

"Jivaka, I am very ill. My body is sick and my mind is even worse. I don't think there is any physician, medicine, or magic that can cure my illness. I am in bed day and night worrying, anguishing, moaning and crying. Jivaka, you may be the most famous physician in the world, yet even you cannot save my life this time."

Jivaka replied seriously, "Your Majesty, do no be sad with despair. There is one person in this world, who can cure your body and mind: the Buddha. I am quite certain there is no other person who can."

All the courtiers were fearful at the mention of the Buddha's name. They were afraid that the king would get angry with Jivaka. The king quietly closed his eyes. Jivaka said with heartfelt understanding, "Your Majesty, I am a physician. A physician can cure physical illness, but I am helpless in treating the sicknesses of the mind. The Buddha is the greatest physician in the world. If your Majesty is willing, the Buddha will welcome your visit. The Buddha is like a great ocean into which all the rivers and streams merge. Your Majesty's misery originates from your mind. To cure the illness of the body, one must first cure the sickness of the mind."

King Ajatsatru agreed, "Jivaka, you are right. I would like to go to see the Buddha, but I am afraid the Buddha may not wish to see me because of what Devadatta and I have done."

Jivaka knew what was weighing heavily on the king's conscience. He went on and said, "Your Majesty, regarding your guilt, I have heard that your father had forgiven you on his death bed. Your father was one of the Buddha's disciples and he has forgiven you. Of course, the all-virtuous Buddha, with his great compassion and love for all beings will forgive you. The Buddha's compassion and kindness are limitless and boundless, and are bestowed graciously on all sentient beings. He does not discriminate or differentiate between the rich and poor. The Buddha allowed Prince Bhadrika and his followers to join the monks but also allowed the poor Upali to ordain. The Buddha accepts alms from the wealthy elder, Sudatta but also accepts offerings from the poor. He was able to convince the incorruptible Mahakasyapa to join the monks, but he also expediently persuaded the greedy Nanda to become a monk. The

Buddha converted Hariti and Angulimalya, whose names frightened all who heard them. He sees everyone just as he sees his son Rahula. Your Majesty, please, you must not hesitate. The Buddha and his disciples are presently teaching the Dharma at my estate. I do hope Your Majesty will go quickly to see the Buddha so that you may eliminate the dark clouds from your mind and return it to being as clear and brilliant as the sunny sky. I implore Your Majesty not to miss this once in a lifetime opportunity."

After listening to Jivaka's eloquent words, the king's eyes shined with hope and regret, "I am very glad to hear what you have just said. You should choose a favorable time and date for me to go to see the Buddha to seek repentance."

Jivaka calmly shook his head, "Your Majesty, according to the Buddha's teachings, there is no such superstition as favorable time and date. The Buddha always instructs his disciples not to seek divination for good or bad omens. Any moment is a favorable moment to study and practice the teachings. Your Majesty, we must leave immediately."

King Ajatasatru was very glad, he gathered a large supply of alms-food and left with an army of servants in an impressive procession for Jivaka's estate.

One the way, King Ajatasatru felt very anxious and afraid. With encouragement from Jivaka, the entourage finally arrived at his estate.

King Ajatasatru said, "Lord Buddha, please see and know my intention."

The Buddha opened his eyes and replied kindly, "Your Majesty, I am glad you have come, I have been waiting for you for a long time."

King Ajatasatru was surprised by this prompt acceptance

and knelt down instantly, bowed his head shamefully and said, "Compassionate and merciful Buddha, I am flattered. A guilty person like me should be glad to receive a scolding from one such as yourself. Instead I am being received with kindness. I am very grateful for your universal love. I now realize that the Buddha's compassion extends equally to all. The Buddha is a father to all sentient beings. I intensely regret that I killed my innocent father. I beg you to be kind and relieve me from my physical and mental suffering."

The Buddha said slowly, "In this world there are two kinds of people who are bestowed with true happiness and good fortune. There are those who cultivate what is wholesome and shun what is unwholesome, and there are those who commit wrongdoing but seek repentance. Your Majesty, now is the time for you to repent and reform. To make mistakes is human. As long as you recognize your mistakes and correct them, you can still realize the Way. The Dharma is limitless; you must repent constantly.

"Your Majesty, unwholesome deeds do not develop naturally, they originate in the mind. When your mind is steadfast in cultivating virtue and abandoning all unwholesome thoughts, then unwholesome deeds will disappear. Once you understand that both your mind and unwholesomeness itself are impermanent, then you will have truly repented. In the years to come you must rule with right teachings and discard incorrect ways. You must win the people over with virtue rather than force. When you govern with charity and benevolence, your reputation for kindness and benevolence will be known far and wide, and you will be respected by all."

"From now on, it is imperative that you reform and behave benevolently and kindly to rid yourself of the anguish in your mind. Then you will find happiness. Further, you must learn the teachings that transcend the mundane and cultivate to attain what is beyond the worldly. By doing so, you will be liberated."

As the Buddha finished speaking, King Ajatasatru was filled with confidence and hope. He felt happy and blessed. The dark clouds over his head dispersed. He was so grateful that he knelt in front of the Buddha and wept.

GLOSSARY

Ajatasatru, King: King of Magadha during the time of the Buddha that rose to power by killing his father, King Bimbisara. Later in life King Ajatasatru became a follower and patron of the Buddha.

Ananda: One of the ten great disciples of the Buddha. He is known as foremost in hearing and learning.

Aniruddha: One of the ten great disciples of the Buddha. He is known as foremost of those who had attained the celestial eye.

arhat: A noble person who has eliminated all afflictions and is no longer subject to rebirth.

asura: One variety of celestial beings. They are angry and jealous beings who are constantly at war with others.

Bamboo Grove: A monastery outside the city of Rajagrha given to the Buddha and his sangha by King Bimbisara.

Bimbisara, King: King of Magadha during the time of the Buddha. He was a devout Buddhist and a major patron of the sangha.

bodhisattva: One who seeks to attain Buddhahood and liberate all sentient beings.

Brahman: The priest caste of ancient India. The term "Brahman" can refer both to priests of the pre-Hindu Brahmanical religion as well as those born from the Brahman caste of any religion.

Buddha: An awakened one. The term "the Buddha" most often refers to the historical Buddha, Sakyamuni Buddha.

Buddha nature: The inherent nature of all sentient beings that is pristine and pure and allows them the opportunity to become awakened.

declining Dharma: An era after the Buddha's parinirvana when awakening will be very difficult to attain.

Dependent Origination: See "Twelve Links of Dependent Origination."

Devadatta: Monk during the time of the Buddha who tried to usurp leadership of the sangha from the Buddha, making numerous attempts on his life.

Dharma: The teachings of the Buddha, the ultimate truth.

Dharma wheel: A symbol of the Buddha's teachings. The Dharma wheel rolls forth, crushing all delusions and afflictions. Its roundness is meant to symbolize perfection.

eight difficulties: Eight possible rebirths in which it is difficult to see the Buddha or hear the Dharma: rebirth in hell, rebirth as a hungry ghost, rebirth as an animal, rebirth where one is always comfortable, rebirth in heaven, rebirth as one with impaired faculties, rebirth as a sophist, and rebirth when the previous Buddha's teachings have faded and a future Buddha has not yet arisen.

emptiness: The concept that everything in the world arises due to dependent origination and has no permanent self or substance.

five aggregates: Form, feelings, perception, mental formations, and consciousness. Five things the Buddha identified as not possessing a self.

four elements: Earth, water, fire, and wind. The four elements that make up everything in the world.

Four Noble Truths: A fundamental and essential teaching of Buddhism that describes the presence of suffering, the cause of suffering, the cessation of suffering, and the path leading to the cessation of suffering.

gandharva: One variety of celestial beings. They are musicians in the court of Sakra-devanamindra.

garuda: One variety of celestial beings. They are mighty bird-like creatures with powerful wings.

Jetavana Monastery: A monastery outside of the city of Sravasti donated to the Buddha and his sangha by the Elder Sudatta and Prince Jetakumara. The Buddha spent the rains retreat here more years than in any other monastery.

Jivaka: The most celebrated physician during the time of the Buddha. He was a devout Buddhist and would treat members of the sangha when they were ill.

kalpa: An inconceivably long unit of time used in ancient India.

Kapilavastu: The kingdom where the Buddha was born.

karma: All wholesome and unwholesome actions, speech, and thoughts and their effects.

Kasyapa Buddha: The Buddha that arose in the world before our present Buddha, Sakyamuni Buddha.

kinnara: One variety of celestial beings. They are celestial musicians that are half-human and half-horse.

Kausala: A kingdom during the time of the Buddha north of the Ganges River. Its major city was Sravasti.

Magadha: A kingdom during the time of the Buddha south of the Ganges River. Its capital city was Rajagrha.

Mahakasyapa: One of the ten great disciples of the Buddha. He is known as foremost in ascetic practices.

Mahayana: One of the main traditions of Buddhism. Mahayana Buddhism stresses that helping other sentient beings attain awakening is as important as self-liberation.

mahoraga: One variety of celestial beings. They are giant serpent-like creatures.

Maudgalyayana: One of the ten great disciples of the Buddha. He is known as the foremost in possessing supernatural powers, and the foremost in filial piety.

merit: Blessings that occur because of wholesome deeds.

Middle Way: The path between the extremes of hedonism and extreme asceticism taught by the Buddha.

Mt. Sumeru: The largest mountain in existence. Located at the center of the world in Buddhist cosmology.

naga: One variety of celestial beings. They are dragon-like creatures that are often benevolent.

Nirgrantha: One of the sects of wanderers during the time of

220

the Buddha. They survive today as the followers of the Jain religion.

Prasenajit, King: King of the kingdom of Kausala during the time of the Buddha.

pratyekabuddha: Those who awaken through their own efforts without having heard the teachings of a Buddha.

precepts: Series of Buddhist moral codes, the most common of which are the five precepts: to refrain from killing, stealing, sexual misconduct, unwholesome speech, and consuming intoxicants.

Rahula: The Buddha's son and one of his ten great disciples. Ordained from a young age, he was the first novice monk in the Buddhist sangha.

Rajagrha: Capital city of the kingdom of Magadha which was situated close to Vulture Peak and the Bamboo Grove

refuge: The practice of "going for refuge" to the Buddha, Dharma, and Sangha is the traditional way to signify that one had become a Buddhist.

Sakra-devanamindra: A celestial being that is kind of the heaven of the thirty-three.

sangha: The community of Buddhist monks and nuns.

Sariputra: One of the ten great disciples of the Buddha. He is known as foremost in wisdom.

Seven Limbs of Enlightenment: Mindfulness, investigation of phenomena, diligence, joy, ease, concentration, and equanimity. These seven factors that contribute to awakening were often chanted during the time of the Buddha to relieve illness.

six realms: Six possible destinations of rebirth: the hell realm, the realm of hungry ghosts, the animal realm, the asura realm, the human realm, and the heavenly realm.

Sravasti: Major city in the kingdom of Kausala. Situated near Jetavana Monastery.

Subhuti: One of the ten great disciples of the Buddha. He is known as foremost among those who have penetrated emptiness.

Sudatta: A wealthy elder from the kingdom of Kausala who was a devout lay follower of the Buddha. He was a major patron of the sangha and donated Jetavana Monastery to the Buddha.

Suddhodana: Ruler of Kapilavastu and father of the Buddha.

Suprabuddha: Father of Yasodhara and former father-in-law of the Buddha.

sutra: Scriptures of the teachings of the Buddha.

Three Dharma Seals: All conditioned phenomena are impermanent, all phenomena are without a self, and nirvana is perfect tranquility. Three truths about reality.

three worlds: The desire world, the form world, and the formless world. Human beings reside in the desire world.

Triple Gem: The Buddha, Dharma, and Sangha.

Twelve Links of Dependent Origination: Central Buddhist doctrine that all phenomena arise due to causes. There are twelve links that describe the series of causes by which old age and death arise in the world: Old age and death arise due to birth, birth arises due to becoming, becoming arises due to clinging, clinging arises due to craving, craving arises due to feeling, feeling arises due to contact,

contact arises due to the six sense organs, the six sense organs arise due to name and form, name and form arise due to consciousness, consciousness arises due to mental formations, and mental formations arise due to ignorance.

Upali: One of the ten great disciples of the Buddha. He is known as foremost in knowledge of the monastic rules.

Venerable: Mode of address for monks and nuns to show respect.

Vipasyin Buddha: A Buddha of the past that arose in the world ninety-one kalpas ago.

Vulture Peak: A hill overlooking the city of Rajagrha where the Buddha would often deliver teachings.

Wandering Sect: One of many different religions during the time of the Buddha whose adherents were wandering alms-mendicants. Members of these religions were often at odds with the Buddha. Very few of them have survived to the modern day.

Way, the: The truth.

yaksa: One variety of celestial beings. Yaksas are often malevolent demon-like creatures.

Yasodhara: The former wife of the Buddha and mother of Rahula. She later joined the sangha and became a nun.

ABOUT THE AUTHOR

Founder of the Fo Guang Shan (Buddha's Light Mountain) Buddhist Order and the Buddha's Light International Association, Venerable Master Hsing Yun has dedicated his life to teaching Humanistic Buddhism, which seeks to realize spiritual cultivation in everyday living.

Master Hsing Yun is the 48th Patriarch of the Linji Chan School. Born in Jiangsu Province, China in 1927, he was tonsured under Venerable Master Zhikai at the age of twelve and became a novice monk at Qixia Vinaya College. He was fully ordained in 1941 following years of strict monastic training. When he left Jiaoshan Buddhist College at the age of twenty, he had studied for almost ten years in a monastery.

Due to the civil war in China, Master Hsing Yun moved to Taiwan in 1949 where he undertook the revitalization of Chinese Mahayana Buddhism. He began fulfilling his vow to promote the Dharma by starting chanting groups, student and youth groups, and other civic-minded organizations with Leiyin Temple in Ilan as his base. Since the founding of Fo Guang Shan monastery in Kaohsiung in 1967, more than two hundred temples have been established worldwide. Hsi Lai Temple, the symbolic torch of the Dharma spreading to the West, was built in 1988 near Los Angeles.

Master Hsing Yun has been guiding Buddhism on a course of modernization by integrating Buddhist values into education, cultural activities, charity, and religious practices. To achieve these ends, he travels all over the world, giving lectures and actively engaging in religious dialogue. The Fo Guang Shan organization also oversees sixteen Buddhist colleges and four universities, one of which is the University of the West in Rosemead, California.

Other Works by Venerable Master Hsing Yun:
Being Good
Infinite Compassion, Endless Wisdom
Traveling to the other Shore
The Core Teachings
Where is Your Buddha Nature?
Humanistic Buddhism: A Blueprint for Life
Chan Heart, Chan Art
Humble Table, Wise Fare

ABOUT THE PUBLISHER

As long as Venerable Master Hsing Yun has been a Buddhist monk, he has had a strong belief that books and other documentation of the Buddha's teachings unite us emotionally, help us practice Buddhism at a higher level, and continuously challenge our views on how we define our lives

In 1996, the Fo Guang Shan International Translation Center was established with this goal in mind. This marked the beginning of a string of publications translated into various languages from the Master's original writings in Chinese. Presently, several trans-lation centers have been set up worldwide. Centers that coordinate translation or publication projects are located in Los Angeles and San Diego, USA; Sydney, Australia; Berlin, Germany; Argentina; South Africa; and Japan.

In 2001, Buddha's Light Publishing was established to publish Buddhist books translated by the Fo Guang Shan International Translation Center as well as other valuable Buddhist works. Buddha's Light Publishing is committed to building bridges between East and West, Buddhist communities, and cultures. All proceeds from our book sales support Buddhist propagation efforts.